Europe finds the World

Trevor Cairns

ART EDITORS BANKS AND MILES

CAMBRIDGE UNIVERSITY PRESS

CAMBRIDGE

LONDON · NEW YORK · MELBOURNE

Paintings and drawings by Zena Flax
Diagrams by Banks and Miles
Maps by Reg Piggott

Published by the Syndics of the Cambridge University Press
The Pitt Building, Trumpington Street, Cambridge CB2 1RP
Bentley House, 200 Euston Road, London NW1 2DB
32 East 57th Street, New York, NY 10022, USA
296 Beaconsfield Parade, Middle Park, Melbourne 3206,
  Australia

© Cambridge University Press 1973

Library of Congress Catalog Card Number: 70–111126
ISBN 0 521 04422 7

First published 1973
Reprinted 1975

First printed in Great Britain by
Jarrold and Sons Ltd, Norwich
Reprinted in Great Britain by Cox and Wyman Ltd,
London, Fakenham and Reading

front cover: Aztec shield, decorated with feather
mosaic. Feathers were woven into, or stuck to, stout
fabric, and the whole then mounted on wood and
leather. The most elaborate shields were probably used
only in ceremonies. The diameter of this shield is
$29\frac{1}{2}$ in (75 cm).

back cover: One of a pair of late sixteenth-century
Japanese screens, standing 5 ft (152 cm) high, showing
a Portuguese ship arriving. The merchants and sailors,
brightly clad with tall hats and wide pantaloons, are
awaited by black-robed missionaries. All these foreigners
arrived from the south, so the Japanese term for
paintings of this type is Namban which means
Southern Barbarian.

title page: A terrestrial globe made in 1599 by the
famous Dutch cartographer Willem J. Blaeu. The
wooden frame is of later date.

Illustrations in this volume are reproduced by kind
permission of the following:

Front cover, Würtemburgisches Landesmuseum, Stuttgart;
back cover, Smithsonian Institution, Freer Gallery of Art,
Washington; title page, Crown copyright, Science Museum,
London; pp. 4, 5, 6, Dean and Chapter of Hereford Cathedral;
p. 7 caravan, Mansell Collection; p. 7 woodcuts, from *The
Book of Spices*, by F. J. Rosengarten Jr, Livingstone Publishing
Co, 1969; pp. 11, 14, from A. C. Moule, *Quinsai*, C.U.P.; p. 12
football players, The Cleveland Museum of Art, gift of Mr and
Mrs W. A. Cowett; p. 12 dove, Setsu Gatodo Co Ltd, Tokyo;
pp. 12 vase, 85 wigstand, 87, 91, Victoria and Albert Museum;
p. 13 silk, Museum of Fine Art, Boston; p. 13 poet and moon,
Hakone Museum, Japan; p. 15, Lilly Library, Indiana
University; pp. 16, 21 compass, 24, 30, 41 diagram, after B.
Landström, *The Ship, The Quest for India* and *Columbus*, Allen
& Unwin; pp. 20, 21 astrolabe, 27 castle, 28, 53 pectoral,
54 skull, 55 knife, 57, 61, 76–7, Trustees of The British Museum;
pp. 21 portolano, 25, Bibliothèque Nationale, Paris; pp. 27
crosses, 41 gun, Museu de Marinha, Lisbon; p. 32, Academia c
Ciências, Lisbon; p. 35 temple, India Government Tourist
Office; pp. 36 stupa, 37, 88 Akbar, 89 feast, washing, weaving,
R. Skelton; pp. 41, 83, National Maritime Museum, London;
p. 43, Ministério do Ultramar, Lisbon; pp. 47 Carib, 48, Anne
Bolt; pp. 47 galley, 51, 58, 66, 80, Radio Times Hulton Picture
Library; p. 50, Peter Wadhams; p. 52, Instituto Nacional de
Bellas Artes, Mexico; p. 53 head-dress, Museum für Völkerku
Vienna; p. 54 Huitzilopochtli, City of Liverpool Museums;
p. 55 rack, Biblioteca Medicea Laurentiana, Florence; p. 59,
United States Information Service; pp. 60, 62, 63, 64, 69 Cuzcc
Anne Kendall; p. 67, Archivo General de Indias, Seville;
p. 68, Foteco-Bolivia; p. 69 Lima, V. Kennett; p. 72 from R.
Cameron, *Viceroyalties of the West*, Weidenfeld & Nicolson;
p. 74, Biblioteca Nacional, Madrid; p. 75, R. A. Gardner;
pp. 84 de Hooch, 85 Steen, Trustees of The Wallace Collection
pp. 84 de Keyser, 85 Hobbema, The National Gallery,
London; p. 86 bedspread, The National Trust; p. 88 Taj
Mahal, Richard Don; pp. 88 mausoleum, 89 General, India
Office Library; pp. 34, 36 Buddha, 39, 73, photo Banks &
Miles; p. 94 after Douville and Casanova, *Daily life in early
Canada*, Allen & Unwin; p. 53 list, Bodleian Library.

Contents

THE HEREFORD MAP
Diameter 52 in (1·3 m), drawn on vellum by Richard de Bello.

A medieval map of the world

In the north aisle of Hereford cathedral there hangs this map. It shows what educated men thought of the world in the thirteenth century, about the end of the Crusades. Though the shape of the continents and countries is not very accurate, it is easy to see that the map-maker knew about them. (The diagram shows the outlines and most important names more clearly.) America and Australia were unheard of, but the other three continents are there, with the Holy Land in the middle.

Placing Palestine and Jerusalem, the Holy City, in the centre of the world suited the religious ideas of medieval people, but it was also reasonable geography, because the Holy Land does lie where the three continents come closest together. Besides, this map was probably made by a churchman for the use of churchmen, which is why so many of the pictures are meant to show where events in the Bible took place. Here are some of them.

Adam and Eve eat the fruit in Eden.

Joseph's granaries – the Pyramids.

The tower of Babel – perhaps a Babylonian ziggurat.

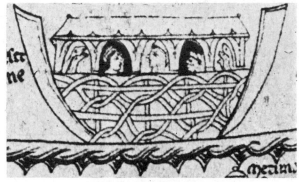

Noah's Ark at rest on Mount Ararat.

Rhinoceros (Egypt).

Mandrake (Egypt).

Norwegian with skis.

Other pictures show some of the strange animals and people who were believed to dwell in far-off places. They may seem fantastic to us, but are they really much more astonishing than some of the animals in the zoo?

It was difficult for anyone who stayed at home to be sure where truth ended and fiction began, especially as some travellers either exaggerated or told outright lies about the lands they claimed to have seen. One of the most famous of these tellers of tall tales called himself Sir John Mandeville. To this day nobody is sure who he was, but he lived in the fourteenth century, supposedly in Flanders. His book was a clever mixture of truth and lies, and was very popular. How far the readers believed it is something we do not know; people read far-fetched things nowadays, and there have been quests for 'lost cities' and 'the abominable snowman'.

It would be a bad mistake to think that educated people in the Middle Ages were easily taken in, and would swallow any nonsense. Even though their maps were out of shape, many men had a coldly practical knowledge of other parts of the world, especially Asia. There were wandering mercenaries, soldiers of fortune. There were pilgrims to the Holy Land who wrote guide books for the use of other pilgrims. Above all, there were the missionaries and the merchants.

Blemye (Africa).

Mermaid (Mediterrane

Bactrian camel (Asia).

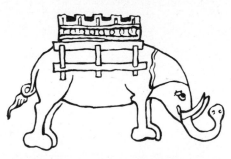

Elephant with castle (India).

Sciapod (Asia).

1. MEDIEVAL CONTACTS WITH THE FAR EAST

The roads of silks and spices

Ginger 1492.

Cloves 1487.

If you already know about life in the Middle Ages, you will remember that meat or fish had often been dead for a long time before it reached the table. If it had not begun to go bad, this would be because it had been thoroughly smoked or salted – there were no other methods of preserving. Many people today like well-seasoned food, so imagine how keen people were to have spicy sauces then, when the taste of the meat or fish sometimes needed to be disguised.

Bottles of sauce often have on their labels lists of the ingredients from which they have been made. Look at such a list next time you have a chance, and see how many eastern spices have been used, spices which are still mainly grown in the Far East.

Carrying goods from so far away in those times was difficult; it was worth doing only for articles which were both small and valuable. Silk and jewels, besides spices, came from the East. These usually had to be paid for in gold and silver, as Europe did not produce many goods that were sufficiently valued in the East to be worth the cost of transport.

Silks and spices, gold and silver; a trade that could bring great wealth to the men who conducted it. Again, you should remember what you know about the Middle Ages. Merchants became more important and their towns grew in riches and strength. The trading cities of Italy became some of the greatest. The upper map on page 8 will remind you. It shows where the merchants of Venice and Genoa had their main depots and warehouses, where they bought goods which had come in the camel caravans of eastern merchants and loaded them into the holds of their ships.

Camel caravans played the most important part in transporting Eastern spices to Western kitchens. The spices and kitchen are illustrated in early German printed books, the camel and merchants in an Egyptian manuscript, A D 1236.

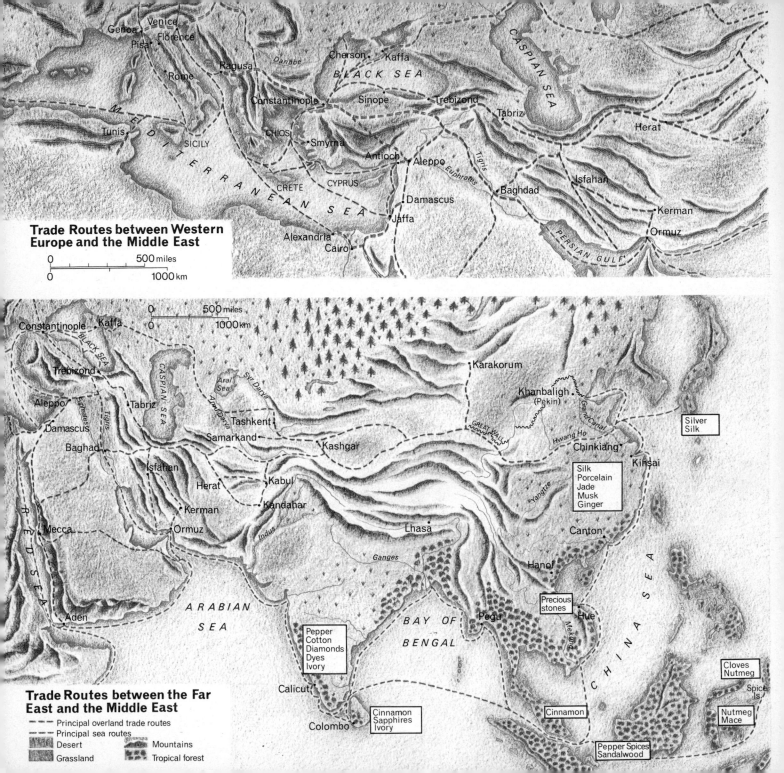

Trade Routes between Western Europe and the Middle East

0 — 500 miles
0 — 1000 km

Genoa · Venice · Florence · Pisa · Rome · Ragusa · Tunis · SICILY · Constantinople · CHIOS · Smyrna · CRETE · CYPRUS · Antioch · Aleppo · Damascus · Jaffa · Alexandria · Cairo

Danube · Cherson · Kaffa · *BLACK SEA* · Sinope · Trebizond · Tabriz · *CASPIAN SEA* · Herat · *Tigris* · *Euphrates* · Baghdad · Isfahan · Kerman · Ormuz · *PERSIAN GULF*

MEDITERRANEAN SEA

Trade Routes between the Far East and the Middle East

0 — 500 miles
0 — 1000 km

Constantinople · Kaffa · *BLACK SEA* · Trebizond · Aleppo · Damascus · Baghad · *Euphrates* · *Tigris* · Tabriz · *CASPIAN SEA* · Isfahan · Herat · Kerman · Mecca · Ormuz · *RED SEA* · Aden

Aral Sea · *Syr Darya* · *Amu Darya* · Tashkent · Samarkand · Kabul · Kandahar · *Indus* · Kashgar · Karakorum · Khanbaligh (Pekin) · *GREAT WALL* · *Grand Canal* · *Hwang Ho* · Chinkiang · Kinsai · Canton · Hanoi · Hue · *Yangtze* · *Mekong* · Lhasa · *Ganges* · Pegu

ARABIAN SEA · *BAY OF BENGAL* · Calicut · Colombo · *CHINA SEA*

Silver / Silk

Silk / Porcelain / Jade / Musk / Ginger

Precious stones

Pepper / Cotton / Diamonds / Dyes / Ivory

Cinnamon / Sapphires / Ivory

Cinnamon

Cloves / Nutmeg · *Spice Is.*

Nutmeg / Mace

Pepper Spices / Sandalwood

- - - Principal overland trade routes
— — Principal sea routes
Desert
Grassland
Mountains
Tropical forest

The caravans had toiled for months, even years, across barren steppes and deserts, over hills and mountains, enduring hunger and thirst, baking heat and paralysing cold. If they were able to survive these hardships and the dangers of disease and accident, they still had to face man-made difficulties. Nomads might kill or rob, or at least extort blackmail. The rulers of the cities which lay on the route, in the more fertile parts of Central Asia, would give refreshment and shelter, but at a price. No wonder spices and silks were expensive.

Sometimes the goods had come only the last part of their journey by caravan, as the next map shows. Sea transport ought to be comparatively cheap, because of the amount that a ship can stow in its hold, but this particular route was exposed to so many dangers and delays that the silks and spices were just as expensive by the time they reached their European buyers.

In the thirteenth century conditions became rather easier on the overland route. This was when the Mongol Empire which had been founded by the mighty Jenghiz Khan was at its height. Under the fourth of the Great Khans, Kublai, who ruled from 1260 to 1294, the empire included China, and there was a certain amount of law and order over the whole vast expanse shown on the map below. Travellers with a safe-conduct from the Khan could feel reasonably secure, and a number of Europeans journeyed into Asia. Some went there for religious or political reasons, some merely to make money.

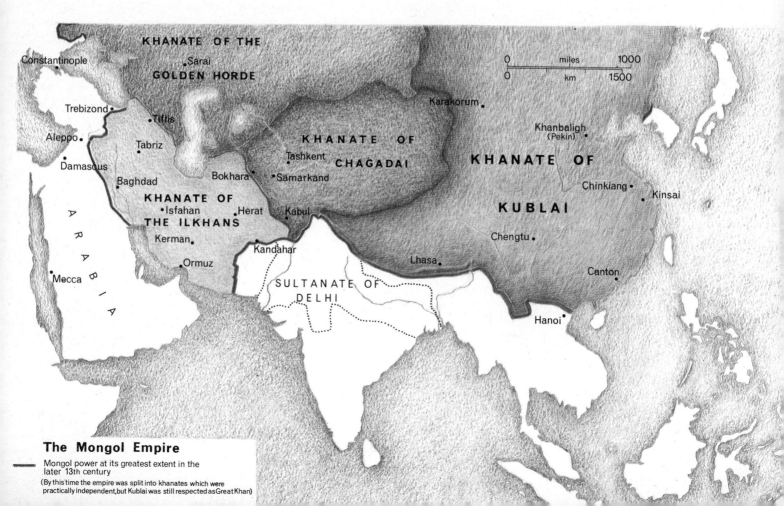

The Mongol Empire

Mongol power at its greatest extent in the later 13th century

(By this time the empire was split into khanates which were practically independent, but Kublai was still respected as Great Khan)

Diplomats and missionaries

For centuries there had been tales in Europe that far away, beyond the lands of the Muslims, there lived a mighty Christian priest-king; his name was Prester (priest) John. In fact, there were many Christians scattered all over Asia, Nestorian Christians as they are called, who had been out of touch with the Christians of the West for many centuries. There were Nestorians in India and China, and some of the Mongol tribes were Nestorians too. Now the Prester John legends took on fresh importance. Would the Great Khan turn out to be this hero? Even if he was not, would he attack the Muslims from the East while the kings of Europe launched a new crusade?

At different times several ambassadors travelled between West and East to discuss plans of this sort. For example, in 1245 the Pope sent Friar John Carpini to the Great Khan, and in 1253 King Louis IX of France sent Friar William Rubruck; in 1287 the khan who ruled in Persia sent Rabban Sauma, a Nestorian priest from China, to the Pope and the kings of France and England. None of the proposed alliances, however, came into effect.

Other priests travelled on purely religious business. Friar John of Monte Corvino, for instance, went to Pekin, and remained there as archbishop for about forty years. Not long before his death in 1328 he was visited by another friar, Oderic of Pordenone, who has left a description of his travels.

Merchants

The most famous account of the Far East and the routes there was not written by a priest, but by a Venetian merchant. Between 1255 and 1269 the brothers Niccolo and Maffeo Polo travelled to China and back. In 1271 they set off again, this time with Niccolo's seventeen-year-old son Marco. We shall have more to say about Marco's description of China. But the Polos were by no means the only merchants to be eastern experts. Francesco Pegolotti, who worked at the Genoese trading depot at Kaffa on the Black Sea, wrote a handbook, about 1340, explaining how to carry on trade with the Far East.

Perhaps the most daring of all were the Vivaldi brothers of Genoa. They believed that it should be possible to take ships all the way round Africa, and so come to India and China. In 1291 they sailed through the Straits of Gibraltar to find the sea route to the East. No more is known.

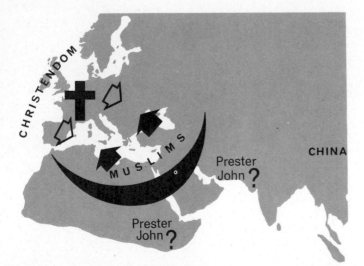

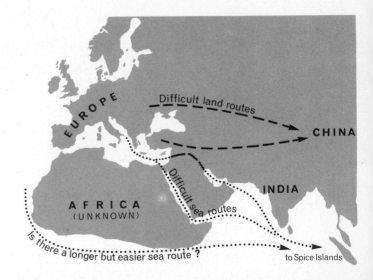

China in the time of Kublai Khan

The Polos took three years and a half on their second journey to China. Kublai Khan was pleased to see the two older men again, and soon formed a high opinion of young Marco. He employed Marco on many tasks in different parts of China, often asking him to inspect and report on what was happening in various provinces. In this way Marco Polo learned much about China, and greatly admired it.

We can understand his admiration if we know even a little of what he said about the city of Kinsai; that it was noble, magnificent, the greatest and most beautiful in the world, and so full of delights that it deserved its title of 'the heavenly city'. It has been possible to check many of the things which Marco Polo described, from books written by other Europeans like Oderic of Pordenone and especially from writings of the Chinese themselves; though Marco made some mistakes, on the whole he was very accurate. The city stood between the river, which was crowded with merchant ships, and a very beautiful lake. The inner ramparts were about eleven miles long, and had five gates for canals and thirteen for roads. The outer ramparts were over eighteen miles long, but we are not sure if they encircled the city or only protected the weakest sides. The Chinese census figures of that time give the number of families, not individuals, but they are enough to show that the visitors who guessed at a population of a million were correct. There were ten main markets, each held three days a week and attended by forty or fifty thousand people. In spite of the enormous crowds, the city was kept very clean; streets were swept and cess-pits emptied regularly. The streets were paved with large flagstones; the main one, the Imperial Way, was sixty yards wide. The canals were crossed by hundreds of bridges, and were railed off to prevent people – especially drunkards at night – from falling in. These are only some of the bare facts about the city of Kinsai, but they are enough to suggest comparisons with the cities of Europe during the Middle Ages.

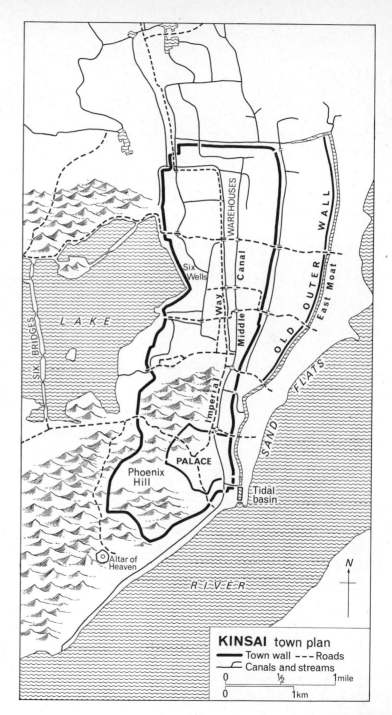

KINSAI town plan
— Town wall --- Roads
⊏ Canals and streams

0 ½ 1 mile
0 1 km

below: Football players,
painted about the time of Kublai.

This fourteenth-century
porcelain vase shows a
scene from a play written
in the time of the Mongol
emperors. Two lovers are
near a summer-house in
the grounds of a temple.

below: Dove on a branch
of peach blossom,
painted by the Emperor
Hui-tsung (1082–1135).

To get an idea of the nature of Chinese civilisation, of the tastes of the upper classes at least, look carefully at the pictures on these two pages. What do you think of the people who painted them or enjoyed looking at them? Were they clever or stupid? Hard or soft? Thoughtful or rash? Delicate or clumsy? Had they any sense of humour? What did they feel about the people in the paintings? Or about nature – trees, mountains, rivers, flowers? It is not wise to try to make up your mind about a civilisation entirely from the art it produces, but you can pick up a quick impression. Even if far from being the whole truth, often it is roughly accurate.

below left: Ladies preparing silk, also by Hui-tsung, copying an eighth-century painting. The ladies are pounding the cloth to thicken it.

below: Poet looking at the moon, by the court painter Ma Yuan (fl. 1190–1224). A servant waits quietly while his master is inspired by natural beauty.

Part of the river and town at Kinsai, from a nineteenth-century copy of a plan drawn in 1274.

Waterways of China

Canals ⌐⌐⌐⌐ Rivers ～～
Great wall ～～～
0 miles 500
0 Km 800

Behind the refined culture lay hard work and practical ability. The peasants, as in all lands, had to work hard, but in China the government had often added to their labour by making them help to build fortifications and canals. You know about the Great Wall, and have probably also heard of the Grand Canal; the map shows the Chinese waterways which, as far as we can tell, were navigable in Marco Polo's time. There were inventions which Europe did not copy for many years; printing had been well developed in China by the tenth century AD. This had combined with the banking system of their merchants to produce printed credit notes and at last, a few years before Marco Polo's visit, printed paper money. The Chinese were also aware of how a magnetised needle would point north–south, though they seem to have known of this for centuries before it occurred to them to use it for navigation. They knew of that explosive chemical which we call gunpowder; that would be a bad name for it here, though, as the Chinese did not use it in guns, but more in fireworks.

An empire like this obviously needed very able men to run it, and for well over a thousand years there had been a highly organised Civil Service. These men, under the emperor, ruled the land; they governed towns, districts, whole provinces. To become one of them, and to get the chance of rising to become an extremely powerful mandarin, a young man had to sit a series of very stiff examinations. If he passed (and most failed) his starting position in the Civil Service could depend on how good his results were. The examinations were very fair, and so was the promotion system once a man was in the Civil Service, though sons and grandsons of officials naturally had an advantage. All the same, any educated young man had a chance.

The key to a government job was education in the Chinese classical books, and by studying the same books all the officials had learned the same ways of thinking, the same attitudes. Some of these ideas were very good, especially those which were the teachings of Confucius. He had lived as long ago as 550–480 BC, approximately, and had taught that men should think clearly and behave with justice and kindness. 'Treat others as you wish to be treated yourself' was his main teaching; this is easy to say, not so easy to work out in practice, and the wise sayings and practical advice of Confucius had been collected into a book which every educated Chinese knew. Confucius was not a religious leader, and people of any religion could follow his advice. It may well be that the high standards and steadiness of the men who ruled China came largely from their study of Confucius.

There were some disadvantages, however. There was a habit of despising other people. This may have been one reason why the laws of China were so severe, for the criminals deserved punishment just as much as the good deserved reward. Certainly the governing classes of China despised soldiers, regarding them as brutal, violent and blood-thirsty men, hardly different from criminals. They also believed that, compared to the Chinese, other nations were rude and backward.

Despising warriors and foreigners had not saved China from civil wars and invasions and conquests; there, it may seem, was the weakness. Yet Chinese civilisation went on, in spite of all disasters. Think of what happened to any of the other civilisations you know about, and you will appreciate the strength of the Chinese. Kublai Khan the Mongol, though he conquered most of China, valued the civilisation and did not destroy it. Though he served Kublai Khan, Marco Polo wrote with astonished admiration, not about Mongol civilisation, but about Chinese.

After many years in the service of Kublai, the Polos wished to return to their own land. At first the khan was unwilling to let them go, but at last he was persuaded to place them in command of a fleet carrying a princess to marry the khan of

400-wen note issued under Kublai, from a Chinese illustration measuring 8×3½ in (20×9 cm).

A mandarin sitting in judgment. He writes on his scroll with a brush, while an ink palette and spare brush are ready to hand. Before him stand the handcuffed prisoners, with two guards and a jailer. Rods and cords lie on the floor in case torture is necessary. A sixteenth-century picture but typical over many centuries.

15

The north European type of ship showed Viking ancestry in its hull shape, clinker build and single 'steerboard'; but it was larger and bulkier, carried 'castles', was rarely rowed. This reconstruction is based on English seals of the thirteenth century.

A Mediterranean merchant ship, drawn from thirteenth-century Italian carvings. The hull with its twin steering paddles harked back to classical Rome, but the lateen sails had probably been copied from the Arabs.

A large Chinese junk. This type was well known in the nineteenth century, but seems to correspond closely to the type described by Marco Polo. The large rudder is concealed below the water, but the battens stiffening the sails are obvious.

Persia (the same man who had sent Rabban Sauma to Europe, as you read on page 10). They sailed in 1292, and took two years to reach Persia. When Marco described the sort of ships used in the Indian trade, with their sixty or more private cabins and their water-tight bulkheads (things unknown in European vessels for centuries to come), he was speaking from experience. He might have added that the flat, stiffened sails of the junks were much more efficient than the baggy sails of Europe at that time.

In 1295 the Polos came home. Marco never went back to China. We cannot tell whether he wished to; whether he thought that Chinese civilisation was better than that of Europe or not; whether East and West could learn from each other, or whether he simply accepted that different peoples live in different ways. Soon after his return to Venice he was made captain of a ship in a war against the rival city of Genoa, was taken prisoner and spent three years before being released. It was during this time that he wrote his book. Some people believed him, but some could not believe that the Far East could possibly be as vast and splendid as he said it was. They nicknamed him 'Marco Millions'.

Contact is broken

These journeys of merchants and priests might have developed into a regular friendly exchange between Europe and the Far East. Instead, they were roughly ended.

The main reason for this was that the Mongol Empire broke up, as you can see. The khans of the different parts of the empire ceased to obey the Great Khan, and travel became as hazardous as before. From out of the disorder and wars there arose another great Mongol conqueror, Timur the Lame, or Tamerlane. He slaughtered and destroyed from the borders of China to the shores of the Mediterranean, and marked the sites of his battles with pyramids of human heads. Among the people he defeated were the Turks, and this gave some hope to Christian kings, but Timur was himself a devout Muslim and would never go out of his way to help Christians. After his death in 1405 his empire shrank, and the great power of the Turks spread more and more across the Middle East.

Meanwhile, in China itself the Chinese drove out the Mongol khans in 1368 and set up a new dynasty of Chinese emperors, the Mings. These thought that China was better off without foreign ideas, and discouraged Christianity.

Spices and silks still came through the old routes, where the caravans still walked, but monks and merchants from the West no longer travelled with them.

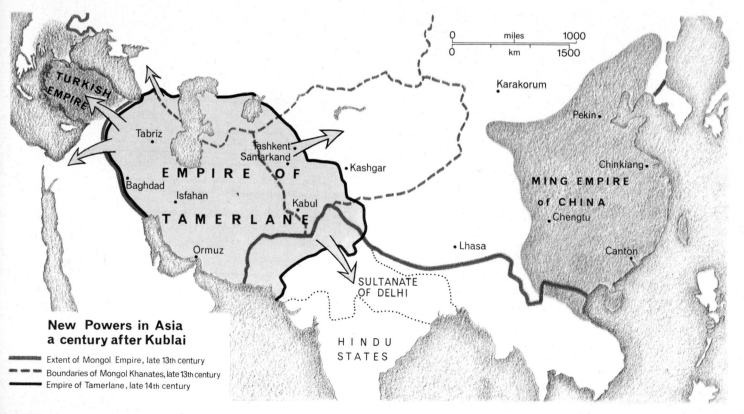

**New Powers in Asia
a century after Kublai**

Extent of Mongol Empire, late 13th century
Boundaries of Mongol Khanates, late 13th century
Empire of Tamerlane, late 14th century

2. THE FIRST OVERSEAS EMPIRE
Exploration south

Portugal
This was the position of Portugal at the beginning of the fifteenth century.

To the north lay part of the Spanish kingdom of Castile, and then the stormy waters of the Bay of Biscay. Across the Bay lay lands belonging to the kings of England and France.

Westwards was the Atlantic. A few islands had been found, but no one knew its size nor what lay beyond. Portuguese fishermen were bold and skilful. So were Portuguese merchants. Lisbon was a great port, half-way stage for ships trading between north Europe and the Mediterranean.

To the east lay Castile, largest of the Spanish kingdoms and an old enemy of Portugal. The last attempt of a king of Castile to conquer Portugal had been defeated in 1385 at the battle of Aljubarrota.

Southwards was the Atlantic again, and the Muslim lands of North Africa, the home of the Moors who had once ruled most of Spain and Portugal. Like the Spaniards, the Portuguese had taken centuries to drive the Moors back, pushing them southwards in a long crusade. The Moors had been driven out in 1250, but Portuguese nobles and knights still thought of themselves as crusaders, and the Muslims of North Africa as the great enemy.

Prince Henry and his purposes

Prince Henry of Portugal was born in 1394. Because his mother came from England, you may sometimes hear it said that this explains why he had an interest in the sea. It is a remarkably silly idea. At that time England was not famous for her seamen; anyway, his mother was a princess, not a sailor's daughter.

Although he is known as Henry the Navigator, he was never a sailor. First and foremost he was a crusading knight. In 1415 he helped his father and brothers to capture the Muslim stronghold of Ceuta, and it may have been this which fixed in his mind the idea of carrying on the fight in Africa. Then in 1417 he became Governor of the Order of Christ, an order of crusading knights rather like the Knights of St John or the Teutonic Knights. In pictures of the ships of Portuguese explorers you often see the cross on their flags or sails. It is the badge of the Order of Christ, which paid for many ships and whose knights often commanded them, under the orders of Prince Henry.

Though we cannot be certain of how and why Henry first got the idea of sending ships south along the African coast, we have an explanation of his reasons by a writer who knew Henry. Here is a very much shortened version of what this writer, Azurara, says.

Prince Henry wanted.....

① To do something famous and to satisfy his curiosity

② To gain wealth through trade

③ To get to know as much as possible about the enemy

and...

④ To seek allies in the Crusade

⑤ To make heathens Christian

Sagres *Canary Is.* *C. Bojador*

1. The magnanimity of this prince constrained him always to begin, and lead to a good conclusion, high exploits . . . He desired to know what lands there were beyond the Canary Islands and a cape which was called Bojador, for up to that time no one knew.

2. If in these territories there should be any population of Christians, or any harbour which man could enter without peril, they could bring back to the realm many merchandises at little cost.

3. It was said that the power of the Moors of this land of Africa was very much greater than was generally thought . . . And because every wise man is moved by the desire to know the strength of his enemy, the prince devised means to send his people in quest of information.

4. He desired to know whether in those regions there might be any Christian princes in whom the charity and love of Christ were strong enough to cause them to aid him against these enemies of the Faith.

5. The fifth reason was his great desire to increase the Holy Faith in our Lord Jesus Christ, and to lead to this faith all souls desirous of being saved . . . understanding that man could render the Lord no greater service.

The language may sound rather old-fashioned, but there is nothing difficult in understanding the ideas themselves. We can sum them up in a diagram. It may even seem to you that the ideas are so obvious that many people must have thought of them before. Perhaps they had. But there were very grave difficulties.

The difficulties

Look at a map of Africa in your atlas and try to find Cape Bojador. As Azurara said, no sailor had sailed round it and come back to tell what lay beyond. To European seamen, Bojador had come to be a dead-line; once across it, and your doom was sealed. There were reasons for this dread.

First, it might be impossible to return. The ships most commonly used had only one mast and one square sail. They were unhandy, and depended very much upon having a favourable wind. Now, if currents and winds swept a ship south of Bojador, could it get back again? This, of course, assumed that it had been able to struggle away from unknown reefs and rocks. Most sailors though the risks were not worth taking.

Second, if a ship were to sail safely round the cape, what would it find? As far as anyone knew, the further south one went, the hotter it became. It seemed very likely that it would soon be too hot for Europeans to live. There were tales that the sea to the south was boiling, and that the people on land were black because of the heat.

Even if things were not as bad as that, there was a serious problem facing any sailors on the coast of Morocco. The land was barren, the inhabitants Muslims. How could Christians refill their water-casks?

The worst difficulty of all was probably fear of the unknown. Sailors used to have the reputation of being superstitious; that is not very surprising, for they spent their lives at the mercy of forces which no human strength could match. Some feared that the unknown seas held terrible creatures, gigantic enough to smash any ship and devour its crew. The sea still has many mysteries, and it had many more in the fifteenth century.

Breaking the spell

To overcome these difficulties, Henry had two answers: resolute patience and careful planning. He made his home at Sagres, near Cape St Vincent, and from here he sent out ships, one or two at a time, with orders to explore southwards. Year after year the captains came back without having passed the dreaded Bojador, often trying to make up for their failure by sailing into the Mediterranean and attacking Muslim ships.

Henry would listen to their stories patiently, and send them once more to explore southwards. This went on for twelve years.

In 1433 Gil Eannes, a squire who commanded one of Henry's ships, came back like all the others; he had only gone as far as the Canary Islands, and taken captive some of the pagan natives. Next year Henry sent for him again, and urged him kindly but strongly to make a better attempt this time. Eannes resolved that he would not appear before Henry again unless he had succeeded in his mission. A few months later he did appear before Henry, carrying with him a bunch of flowers. He had gathered them from the African shore, south of Bojador.

The spell was broken, the terror ended. Now it was only a matter of braving the perils of an uncharted, hostile coast where the weak and unskilful would die. These were dangers which the Portuguese sailors were ready to face, and Henry made sure that the voyages were well planned and well equipped. Confident that Henry would give them all the help that was humanly possible, the Portuguese captains began to grope their way steadily along the unending coast of Africa.

The Swedish archbishop Olaus Magnus was an exile in Rome when, in 1555, he had his *History of the Northern Peoples* printed. He included some of the perils which Scandinavian sailors were said to have met in the ocean. This is one of them.

The explorers' tools

One of the most important things a captain needed was a chart to show him how much was known already. Prince Henry persuaded famous map-makers to come to Sagres and to set down the information that his sailors brought back. For many years maps like this, called a *portolano*, had been used in sailing the Mediterranean Sea. They showed the coast so well, as you can see, that a captain could recognise where he was and sail along the coast without piling up his ship on the rocks. Soon there were portolano charts – very different from the sort of map you saw on page 4 – for more and more of the African coast.

To make or use a portolano, a sailor had to be able to tell directions fairly accurately. For this, he could judge by the sun or stars, or even by the direction of the prevailing wind. Most convenient of all was the compass. Though the Chinese may have been the first to use such a device, the mariner's compass had been used by European navigators since the twelfth century.

The thirteenth-century 'Pisan Chart' is the oldest portolano in existence. It is drawn on sheepskin and covers the Mediterranean. The straight lines show the main directions, similar to the later points of the compass; a pilot found the nearest line parallel to the route he wished to follow, and used that bearing with whatever adjustments he thought necessary.

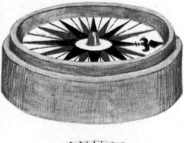

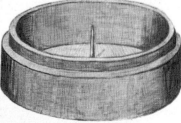

No navigational instruments of this time have been found. The sketch shows the type of compass probably used about 1400, with a card glued to the magnetised arm which was pivoted on a pin. The photograph shows what is probably an Italian astronomer's astrolabe of about 1380; the sea version would have been similar, but simpler and stronger.

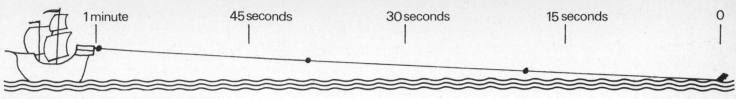

The ship is sailing at a rate of three knots

It was also important to know how far a ship travelled in any particular direction. Sailors had learnt to do this by roughly measuring the speed of the ship. A piece of wood was thrown from the ship into the sea, with a thin rope attached to it. As the ship sailed on, the wood remained bobbing in the water at about the same place; the rope unwound as the ship sailed by and away from the wood. By leaving the wood, or 'log' as English sailors called it, in the water for a minute, say, the seaman would know how far the ship had travelled in that time, and so work out how far it sailed in an hour. In fact it was possible to avoid having to make a calculation each time. To keep our example, if a knot were tied in the rope every one-sixtieth of a mile, all a sailor had to do was to count the knots as he pulled in the rope, and he would know how many miles per hour his ship was travelling. That is why 'knots' is still used at sea when a landsman would say 'miles per hour' or 'kilometres per hour'. Refinements like this, however, came later. Prince Henry's sailors would simply estimate speed by anything floating in the water.

This method of working out a ship's position at sea, using a compass for direction and a log for distance, is called 'dead reckoning'. Though an expert can often be quite accurate with it, there is one big disadvantage. The water of the sea itself is not still, and if ship and log were in a strong current

and the captain did not realise this, bad mistakes could be made.

Naturally, sailors liked to check their position whenever they could, and it was possible for the navigator to find out how far north or south he was by measuring how far the sun or certain stars were above the horizon. For this they used the astrolabe, which had to hang steady and was therefore easier to use on dry land; the cross-staff, where the difficulty was to get the sun and the horizon in your eye at the same moment; and, most simple and practical of all in Prince Henry's time, the mariner's quadrant. When a navigator had read the figure on his scale, he would then look up his almanac which told him the angles of the different stars for different dates and places, as they had been worked out by astronomers. Thus he discovered his latitude.

There is not space here to go into the explanation of such calculations; anyway, you will probably know about them from studying geography. But from what you have seen here you know the sort of instruments that the fifteenth and sixteenth-century explorers used to work out where they were. You may have noticed that we have not said anything about ways of discovering a ship's longitude; there was no satisfactory way of measuring this until the eighteenth century, when a reliable chronometer was first made.

quadrant   cross-staff   astrolabe

Most important of all the explorer's tools was his ship. The design of the hull of the ship can vary according to the job the ship must do. A long ship is faster and easier to steer, cutting through the water. A round ship can carry more and can ride on the water more easily, but is less handy. Then there is height. The 'castles' on a high ship, though good for fighting and helping to save the ship from being swamped by high waves, caught the wind badly. A lower-built ship had less to catch the wind, except the masts and sails which the sailors could alter to suit the weather and their course.

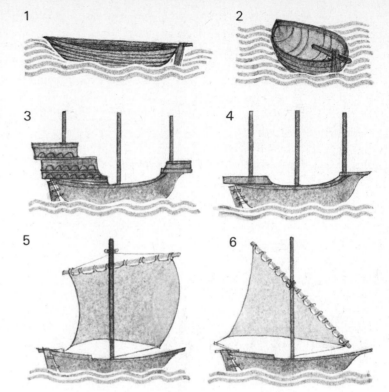

Just as important as the shape of the hull was the shape and position of the sails. The square sails which were usual in Europe were quite good when the wind was pushing steadily from somewhere behind, but they were not easy to turn to catch a sideways wind, partly because of the ship's rigging and partly because the sails themselves were so baggy. For awkward winds, the best sail was the triangular 'lateen' sail, which had been used in the Mediterranean; its usual position was 'fore-and-aft', along the middle of the ship instead of across it.

Then there was the question of where the masts should be put. As you can see from the set of diagrams below, this can make a great difference; do you want your ship to be pushed harder at front, or back, or amidships? Or perhaps you would prefer to be able to alter this to suit yourself, by setting more or less sail in different places? (We assume that you have the sailors to be able to change the sails quickly – the more masts and sails, the more men you are likely to need.)

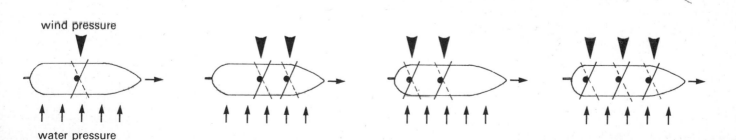

wind pressure

water pressure

When you read about the great explorers, you often see pictures of their ships. Try to decide what the hull and sail design is good for, and what the weak points are. On page 16 you saw shipping of the Middle Ages. Here is a picture of the sort of ship which the Portuguese explorers used in finding their way down the African coast. It was called a caravel, and was developed from the sort of boat which some of the Portuguese fishermen used.

These were the tools of Prince Henry's men. With them, they overcame the difficulties and dangers of unknown currents, uncharted reefs, shoals, rocks. They discovered desert and fertile coasts, grassland and jungle. Every year they added scores or hundreds of miles to the maps. When Henry died in 1460 he had shown the way so well that the king of Portugal himself took charge of the work.

This is how a modern expert reconstructs the Portuguese caravel: low, relatively narrow, with carefully balanced lateen sails. On ocean voyages where the wind could normally be relied upon to blow steadily from a useful angle caravels were sometimes partly rerigged with square sails.

opposite: 'This negro lord is called Musa Mali, Lord of the Negroes of Guinea. So abundant is the gold which is found in his country that he is the richest and most noble lord in all the land.' That is a translation of what is written beside the picture of Mansa Musa in the Catalan Atlas made about 1375. He had in fact died over forty years before, but his fame was so great, and accurate knowledge of Africa was so scanty in Europe, that mapmakers went on including him for decades to come.

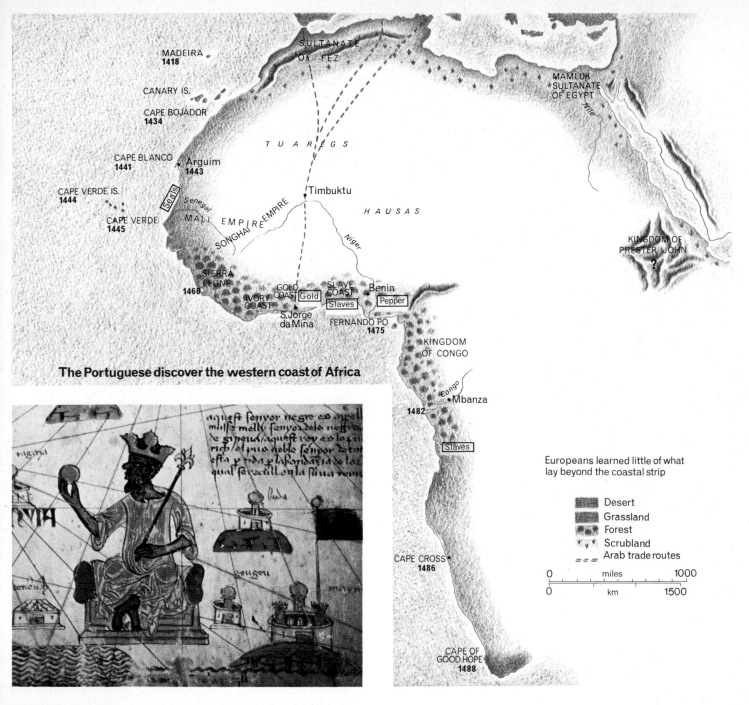

MADEIRA
1418

CANARY IS.

CAPE BOJADOR
1434

CAPE BLANCO
1441

Arguim
1443

CAPE VERDE IS.
1444

CAPE VERDE
1445

SULTANATE
OF FEZ

MAMLUK
SULTANATE
OF EGYPT

Nile

T U A R E G S

Seals

Senegal

Timbuktu

H A U S A S

MALI EMPIRE

SONGHAI EMPIRE

Niger

KINGDOM OF
PRESTER JOHN

?

SIERRA
LEONE
1460

IVORY
COAST

GOLD
COAST

Gold

S.Jorge
da Mina

SLAVE
COAST

Slaves

FERNANDO PO
1475

Benin

Pepper

KINGDOM
OF CONGO

Congo

Mbanza

1482

Slaves

The Portuguese discover the western coast of Africa

CAPE CROSS
1486

CAPE OF
GOOD HOPE
1488

Europeans learned little of what
lay beyond the coastal strip

Desert
Grassland
Forest
Scrubland
- - - Arab trade routes

0   miles   1000
0   km   1500

The beginnings of empire

On the west coast of Africa

One reason for the king's interest in the explorations was simply that they were now showing a profit. Perhaps Prince Henry had expected this, for he must have known about the Muslim merchants and their camel caravans, which had been doing a rich trade across the Sahara for a long time. Gradually the caravels brought to Portugal more and more valuable goods. There was pepper, not as good as the eastern sort, but worth having. There was some gold, and ivory. Possibly the most important came to be the trade in people.

Nowadays we usually think of the West African slave trade as having been one of the foulest crimes in modern history, and some of the most serious problems which face us today can be traced back to it. So it is worth seeing how it started.

At first, Portuguese captains usually got on well with the people they visited. Some Africans willingly went to Portugal and later returned to their own people; Prince Henry hoped that in this way Christianity might be taught. Sometimes Portuguese remained behind when the caravels left, to be picked up the following year. Usually they lived happily with the Africans; one man even made the arduous journey to the great trading city of Timbuktu with African merchants. In these ways the Portuguese were able to learn a great deal about the varied lands and nations of Africa.

Unfortunately, it was not always so peaceful. Some captains were ready to kidnap Africans who trusted them, while some Africans received the strangers with spears and arrows. Either way, prisoners began to be taken to Portugal, where they were sold as slaves. On the whole, they were at first probably treated kindly; they were a novelty, pets rather than beasts of burden. Some Portuguese argued that it was good to bring African slaves to a country where they would learn to be Christians instead of heathens; it gave them a chance of going to Heaven, which they would never have got in their own country, and so it was doing them a very good turn.

Another excuse for taking slaves was that they might have been much worse treated if the Portuguese had not bought them. There were many different African tribes and kingdoms near the Guinea Coast, the main slaving area. In the wars between the kingdoms, captives were taken and these were the people who were often sold to the Europeans. If they had not been sold to the Christians they might have been sold to the Muslims, whose slave-dealers had been trading for many years in Guinea. If they had not been sold at all, they might have been killed. (This may have been true at first, but as the slave trade grew there is little doubt that Africans fought and enslaved one another simply because they knew that they could sell their captives.)

In spite of the excuses, some Portuguese were not happy about the slave trade, especially when it meant splitting up families among different owners. But it went on, and trading posts were set up to collect slaves and any other goods that could be obtained from the local people.

Further south, by the mouth of the Congo, the explorers' discovered that there was one king who ruled over a very wide area from his capital at Mbanza. The king of Portugal in the 1480s and 1490s made friends with the king of the Congo, who became a Christian and welcomed Portuguese settlers and priests into his land. For a time, in the early sixteenth century, it seemed as if an African Christian kingdom of the Congo, helped but not ruled by the Portuguese, would flourish. Unfortunately, the king of Portugal could not send enough help, nor control Portuguese slave-raiders, some of whom even helped cannibal tribesmen to attack the Congo kingdom. Gradually the kings of the Congo lost control over their own people and Christianity faded out.

In Angola, further south still, the Portuguese did not settle until well into the sixteenth century. Here they set themselves up as rulers, and exported slaves in thousands.

Whatever their relations with the nations of the western side of Africa, the Portuguese took care that no other European nation should share in the rich trade which they had opened up. One or two foreign gentlemen were allowed to sail Portuguese ships, like the Venetian merchant Cadamosto in the 1450s, or the Danish knight who disappeared in an African ambush in 1447. But foreign ships were looked upon as trespassers and pirates – and treated accordingly. Like the Carthaginians 2000 years before, the Portuguese had no intention of sharing their trade, and this meant that they kept much of their knowledge secret. The maps and reports of explorers had to be handed in to the Portuguese government as soon as a voyage was over, and instructions and maps for new voyages were carefully prepared and given to the captains shortly before they sailed.

One famous example of care and thoroughness is shown in this picture. The stones from which this castle was built were shaped and numbered in Portugal, so that when they were unloaded on the African coast the parts only had to be fitted together.

Such control and organisation would probably have been worth while for the African trade alone. But Portugal was after something bigger. Already, before his death, Prince Henry had seen the prospect; his successors were moving steadily towards their goal. They were going to open up the sea route to the Far East.

above right: The castle of Sao Jorge da Mina, later known as Elmina, built in 1482 as a fortified trading base on the Gold Coast. The picture is from a Portuguese world chart smuggled out of Lisbon by the Italian Alberto Cantino in 1502 at the risk of his life.

below right: Two *padraos* or stone crosses, now in a Lisbon Museum. That on the left was set up in 1486 at Cape Cross, that on the right at Cape Santa Maria Benguela, then called Cape Agostinho in 1482.

Spying out the eastward route

Now the main concern of the explorers was not to find new parts of Africa, but to find a way round. The continent seemed to go on for ever. There must have been bitter disappointment when, after running eastwards along the Guinea coast, the explorers discovered that the continent stretched south. Still they went on, and by 1486 Diogo Cao, who had reached the Congo a couple of years earlier, had sailed as far south as Cape Cross. That name serves to remind us that the explorers carried with them stone crosses, which they set up at prominent places on the coasts they discovered for Christ and Portugal – you can see the arms of Portugal below the cross. Several of them are still in existence.

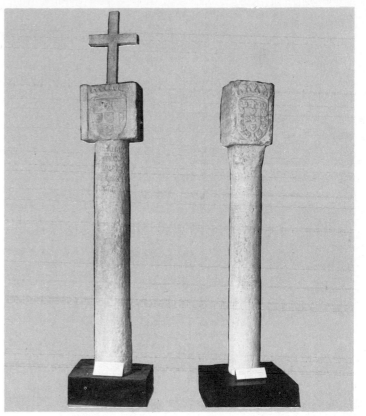

By 1487 the Portuguese government must have judged that the time had come for a final reconnaissance, for they sent out two expeditions in different directions to collect information about the East and the way there.

One of these expeditions went by sea to find the southern tip of Africa and the way beyond. The commander, Bartolomeu Dias, sailed further than any of the others, and then his squadron was caught in savage gales for nearly a fortnight. When the storms abated, Dias steered east in order to find the coast of Africa again. It was not there. He had to steer north before he found it again. He had turned the corner at last. Dias would have sailed further, but his men refused. The ships were battered; provisions were short; they were far from home. Dias returned and reported to the king that he had found the southern corner of Africa, the Cape of Storms as he naturally called it. The king, equally naturally, renamed it the Cape of Good Hope.

The other expedition consisted of only two men, Afonso de Paiva and Pero da Covilha. They were to go overland, travelling in disguise through Muslim lands of North Africa and Asia, where any suspicion that they were really Christian spies would have cost them their lives. The map shows the travels of Covilha. He was with Paiva until they reached Aden, and afterwards travelled alone. At last he made his way back to Cairo, to meet Paiva and return to Portugal. Instead, he learned that his friend had died, and that the king of Portugal would not be satisfied until his agents had visited Prester John. (Such messages were carried by Jewish merchants, who could travel freely through Muslim lands and were not persecuted at this time in Portugal.) Covilha sent his reports on to Portugal, and turned back to visit the land of Prester John, the African Christian kingdom of Ethiopia.

The real Prester John

Ethiopia, or Abyssinia, had been Christian for centuries before the kingdom of Portugal had even existed. Some of the paintings in Ethiopian churches are very similar to those of the Byzantine artists of Constantinople. Shortly before the time of Muhammad, Ethiopia had ruled over part of southern Arabia. In the seventh and eighth centuries however, the vast conquests of the Arabs had driven a huge wedge between Ethiopia and the main Christian centres of Constantinople

and Rome. Contact was practically lost, except that sometimes European pilgrims in the Holy Land would be astonished to meet black-skinned pilgrims, and may have dimly understood that they came from a land far away with a Christian king.

This was a stronger foundation for the Prester John legends than the Nestorian Christians of Asia had provided. Remember Prince Henry's hopes. Would the dream of a grand alliance of Christians, to crush the Muslims by attacking from both sides at once, at last become a reality?

Covilha was well received at the Ethiopian court, and here his wanderings ended. The Ethiopians, partly out of suspicion and partly because they thought that a man of such wide knowledge and powerful intelligence was too valuable to be allowed to leave them, prevented him from returning to Portugal. Messages were sent, and Ethiopian ambassadors visited the king of Portugal, but plans for an alliance were not practical. The Ethiopians were more in need of help against *left:* Some medieval Ethiopian churches are amazingly hewn out of solid rock, and this picture shows an angel making one of them. It measures $13\frac{1}{4} \times 10\frac{7}{8}$ in (33×27 cm) and comes from a mid-nineteenth-century Ethiopian manuscript history. A resemblance to Byzantine art can still be seen.

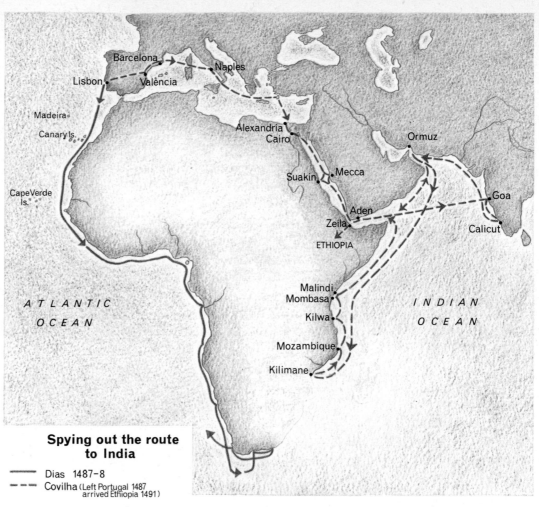

Spying out the route to India

——— Dias 1487–8

- - - - Covilha (Left Portugal 1487 arrived Ethiopia 1491)

the Muslims than able to give it, and most of the kings of Europe were not really interested. The emptiness of the old dream was exposed for the last time.

Years later, other Portuguese visiting the Ethiopian court, after Portugal had secured the sea route to the East and had built forts on the coast of East Africa to guard that route, found Covilha still there. He was treated as an Ethiopian nobleman, and had an Ethiopian wife and family. That is the last that is known of one of the bravest and cleverest explorers in history. Or was he more a spy than an explorer? At any rate, his adventures deserve to be read in detail, though there has not been space to say much about them here.

Sharing the world

With all the reports he had now collected, the king of Portugal could feel sure that he had the sea route to the Far East within his grasp. He was not going to ruin everything by losing his head and rushing at this critical stage. The decisive voyage was prepared carefully and slowly.

Meanwhile Christopher Columbus, a Genoese sailor who had settled in Portugal and had lived for some time on the Azores island of Porto Santo, had come to the king with another idea. Because the world was round, it should be possible to reach the Far East by sailing westwards. Columbus

29

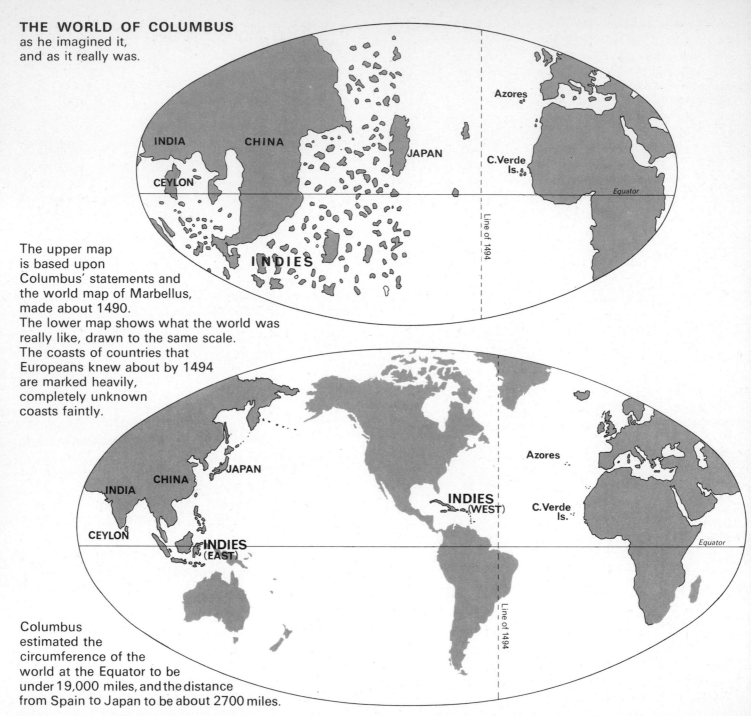

THE WORLD OF COLUMBUS
as he imagined it,
and as it really was.

INDIA   CHINA

CEYLON

JAPAN

Azores

C.Verde
Is.

Equator

Line of 1494

INDIES

The upper map
is based upon
Columbus' statements and
the world map of Marbellus,
made about 1490.
The lower map shows what the world was
really like, drawn to the same scale.
The coasts of countries that
Europeans knew about by 1494
are marked heavily,
completely unknown
coasts faintly.

INDIA   CHINA   JAPAN

CEYLON

INDIES
(EAST)

INDIES
(WEST)

Azores

C.Verde
Is.

Equator

Line of 1494

Columbus
estimated the
circumference of the
world at the Equator to be
under 19,000 miles, and the distance
from Spain to Japan to be about 2700 miles.

wished to sail straight out across the Atlantic until he reached the other side. Here he would find Japan, China and India.

The king turned Columbus down. Columbus thought that the king had cheated by sending out one of his own ships secretly, but the sailors had turned back too soon. Perhaps that did happen; we have no means of knowing. What is more likely is that the Portuguese experts knew that Columbus was badly mistaken about the size of the world, and that no ship could cross an ocean as wide as that which must lie between Europe and the Indies. Besides, if Portugal was sure of finding soon a route round Africa which the Portuguese could hold as their own, why should they look for another route which it would be much harder to prevent other nations from using?

After years of disappointment, Columbus was given his chance by the queen of Spain, and the Portuguese were not pleased when, early in 1493, he came back from the other side of the Atlantic in a Spanish ship, saying that he had found the Indies.

Ferdinand and Isabella, the king and queen of Spain, lost no time in trying to make sure of these newly discovered lands. The safest way of making a claim which everyone would respect, in Christian Europe, was to have it backed by the Pope. Years before, Prince Henry had obtained documents from the Pope giving Portugal the right to all newly discovered lands on the way to India. Now the Spaniards were given a similar document, or Bull as it was called, allowing them the same rights in the West. The Bull was dated 4 May 1493.

This was not exact enough to prevent argument and fighting between Portugal and Spain, and the governments of both countries saw the danger. Therefore a meeting was held in 1494 at the little Spanish town of Tordesillas, and the world was shared out exactly. A line was drawn on the map 370 leagues west of the Azores and Cape Verde islands. Westwards the unknown lands were for Spain, eastwards for Portugal. Obviously, since the world was a globe, the line would have to be continued on the other side of the world when the sailors of the two nations got as far as that.

Had they any right to do this? Was nobody else to have a share? Many people, since those days, have been very indignant. But the truth is that in the 1490s and for many years afterwards no other government in Europe was seriously interested. The Bull and the Treaty of Tordesillas sensibly prevented trouble between the only two kingdoms interested.

As to whether they or anybody else had a right to conquer and rule over the lands and peoples they found, that is a very different question.

The sea way to the East

In Portugal, plans for the great voyage went on. Three ships were specially built, armed and equipped (to the same designs, so that spare parts were interchangeable), also a storeship to go with them, which could be scrapped when its stores had been used. Goods were provided, for trading or presents. Eighteen condemned criminals were to go, too. They would be put ashore to try to make friends with newly found savages; if they survived, they would be given a pardon. All the information which the kings of Portugal had collected over the years was carefully set down for the use of the pilots.

No matter how good the preparations, there would be a tremendous load of responsibility on the commander of the expedition. He must take his squadron thousands of miles away from the slightest chance of help, in unknown seas. When he reached the east coast of Africa, he would find that Muslim Arabs controlled the trade and were settled in the main ports; they would not welcome a stranger who wanted to take some of the trade from them, especially if the stranger turned out to be a Christian. In India it would depend entirely on how the Portuguese impressed the kings of the various kingdoms; they might be received with friendship and respect, or with contempt and enmity.

The king of Portugal picked Vasco da Gama as the best man to solve these problems. Historians have argued as to whether or not it was a wise choice, and it is not fair to try to judge without knowing a lot more about Vasco da Gama than you can read in this book. All the same, it is important to understand what the main arguments are. On the one side, it is said that only a very firm man who was able to be ruthless in times of danger could have led the expedition successfully. On the other hand it is said that Vasco da Gama was needlessly cruel, made enemies instead of friends, and that he and the Portuguese who came after him treated the eastern people they met in such a way that European and Oriental nations find it difficult to trust each other even today.

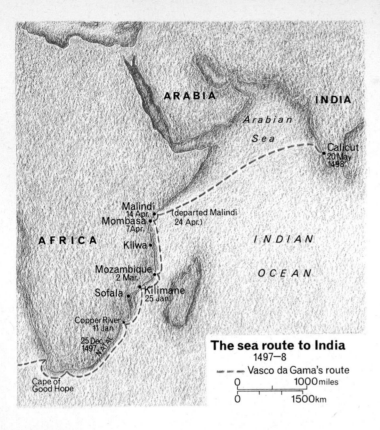

The sea route to India
1497–8
- - - Vasco da Gama's route

0   1000 miles

0   1500 km

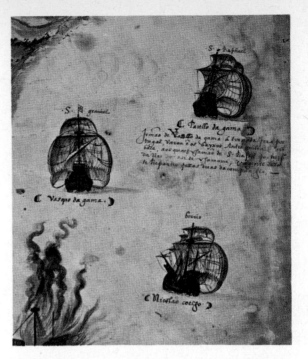

From a mid-sixteenth-century Portuguese manuscript, 'Historia das Armadas', the three ships of Vasco da Gama's fleet, with their names above and their captains' names below. The fourth, a store-ship, was burned when her stores had been used.

Whatever the correct judgment may be, nobody denies that Vasco da Gama was bold and skilful. This map shows how he sailed up the east African coast until he was given a pilot by the ruler of Malindi, and then sailed direct across the Indian Ocean with the monsoon. In May 1498, over ten months after leaving Lisbon, the ships of Vasco da Gama dropped anchor off the Indian city of Calicut.

The trade of the Indian Ocean was at that time mostly controlled by Arab merchants, and the Portuguese knew that they would try to turn the kings of the Indian sea-ports against them. How could Vasco da Gama show the king of Calicut that it was wise to be friendly? He offered gifts, but by Indian standards these were poor, and only made his boasts about the power of Portugal seem like lies. He tried to conceal how weak he was by acting proudly and by saying that other ships were following him; this did not deceive the Indian king, who must have begun to suspect more and more that the Portuguese were spies or pirates, as the Arab merchants said they were. Matters went from bad to worse, hostages were kidnapped on both sides, and at last the Portuguese sailed away from Calicut pursued by a fleet of armed boats.

But Vasco da Gama had not failed. He had opened the sea road to the East. If he had quarrelled with some rulers in East Africa and India, he had made friends with others; indeed, it was almost automatic, for these rulers had friendships and feuds among themselves. He had also found that Portuguese ships and guns were strong enough to overcome anything they were likely to meet in the Indian Ocean.

The way ahead was clear.

India: religions and kings

Rich as he was, the ruler of Calicut was only one of the many who ruled over parts of the Malabar Coast, and this itself was only a part of the gigantic land of India. India was more like a continent than a single country. It was full of different peoples speaking different languages.

India had been the home of civilisations from very ancient times. You may remember that about the same time as the civilisations of the Tigris-Euphrates and Nile valleys, there had been a civilisation in the valley of the Indus; and that when Alexander the Great invaded India, he had to fight the armies of civilised kings. It has even been suggested that one or two of the ideas of Greek philosophers were borrowed from India. The Romans and Byzantines had known the trade routes from the Red Sea before the Arabs made their great advances. During the Middle Ages, priests from Europe sometimes visited the Nestorian Christians who lived in some parts of India. Yet, in spite of these contacts, India and the West had had little effect on each other. You know the saying: 'East is East and West is West'. This was not only because of the great distance between Europe and India, nor the difference in climate; it was largely because of the different ways of thinking about life and death.

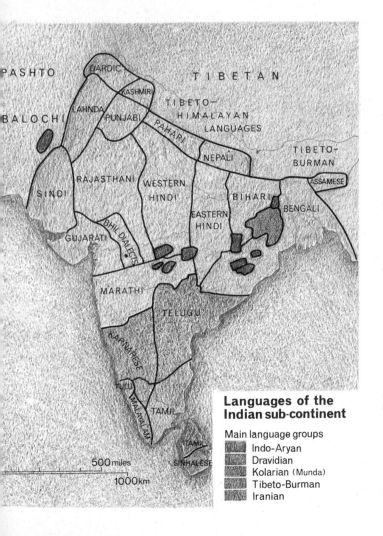

Languages of the Indian sub-continent

Main language groups
- Indo-Aryan
- Dravidian
- Kolarian (Munda)
- Tibeto-Burman
- Iranian

500 miles
1000 km

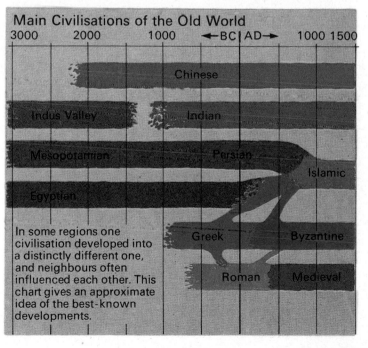

Main Civilisations of the Old World

In some regions one civilisation developed into a distinctly different one, and neighbours often influenced each other. This chart gives an approximate idea of the best-known developments.

The three chief Hindu gods are: BRAHMA, the creator; VISHNU, the preserver; SIVA, the destroyer. Vishnu takes different forms in performing deeds and (*below left*) he is shown boar-headed as he raises the earth goddess from the ocean. He holds his symbols: a mace, a conch shell, a disc; and the two last are also displayed by the small attendants in the bottom corners. Brahma (*left*) and Shiva (*right*) are in the top corners. Shale carving from the Punjab, twelfth century A D, 37 in (94 cm) high.

below centre: Siva can bring wisdom as well as destruction. Here he is Lord of the Dance, surrounded by a circle of flame – the life of the universe – and treading down the dwarf of ignorance. The drum in his upper right hand symbolises creation, the flame in his upper left destruction. His snake-entwined lower right arm bestows protection, and his lower left hand points to his left foot which helps to raise those who worship it. Bronze from Madras, tenth century A D, 26½ in (67 cm) high.

below right: Siva's wife could also be destructive, but here she is in her form of Parvati, kindly mother goddess. Her right hand is raised to hold a flower. Bronze from Madras, thirteenth century A D, 25 in (63 cm) high.

HINDUISM OR BRAHMINISM is the ancient religion of India. It is especially difficult to explain because, over the hundreds and thousands of years, Indians themselves have understood their religion differently. A poor peasant, knowing little outside his own village – most Indians have lived in village communities through the whole of Indian history – would probably not understand his religion in the same way as a highly educated Hindu. For instance, in Hindu temples there are often statues of many gods, and some of them look absurd at first. It may be that some Hindus truly worshipped these strange creatures, but, as the captions explain, there was really a meaning for the shapes and attitudes. Some Hindus believed that the statues represented different gods, while others came to think that they were just different sides of the one great God.

The Hindus believed that the greatest happiness for anyone was to have his soul merged into the great soul of the world – joined with the spirit of God might be another way of putting it. A man's soul would then cease to exist as an individual, he would lose his own personality. This was called *Nirvana*, the final reward of a good man after death. But

In the ruined city of Khajuraho, in central India, stands a famous group of temples built about A D 1000. This is an example. Each room — entrance porch, assembly hall, dancing hall, shrine — has its own domed stone roof. Seen from outside, the roofs carry upwards the worshipper's eyes and thoughts, though the flat discs remind him that his religion belongs to this world as well as to heaven.

only after his *last* death. Men were born many times, and died many times. The wheel of life turned endlessly. There was no escape. As soon as a soul left its dead body, it came again into the body of a new-born baby. The Hindus, then, believed in 'reincarnation'. If a man had lived a good life, he was born next time in a higher state. If he had been bad, he moved downwards; a really bad man could sink down to the lowest of the animals. Among men, there were separate classes or castes. The four main castes which you see in the diagram became subdivided until nowadays there are over 2000, all arranged in order, from highest to lowest. The caste system was very rigid. People could not move during any one life from the caste into which they had been born, and the castes were not supposed to mix and intermarry.

At first glance the caste system may look rather like the division of classes in the West during the Middle Ages, but you soon realise that the whole way of thinking which lay behind each of the two systems was different. Indeed, if you think of all the different civilisations you know about, at any period or place, you are not likely to find another one where the people believed in the final submerging of the individual soul as the ultimate reward of goodness.

If it is difficult for anyone who has been brought up with ideas about the importance of the individual personality to understand the Hindu attitude, it is doubly difficult for anyone who enjoys the ease and comfort which goes with living nowadays in one of the rich industrial countries. Anybody who enjoys life so much that he cannot think of anything worse than death will hardly be able to understand Hinduism. It may be more easily understood by people who have suffered, or seen hardship and misery.

Nirvana

Brahmins

Kshatriyas (warriors)

Vaisyas (craftsmen)

Sudras (peasants)

Animals

A statue of Buddha, 49 in (124 cm) high, carved about AD 1100 in Bengal or Bihar. This is the 'earth-witness' pose. Buddha, wearing a thin robe, tall crown and necklaces, sits on a lotus throne and points to the earth to bear witness to his truth and wisdom. The earth goddess, shown in the centre of the pedestal below, rises up to do so. She carries a jar of treasure, symbol of the earth's plenty.

below left: Buddhists built *stupas* (mounds) for relics of Buddha himself or of his holiest followers. One of the most famous is this, built about 150 BC at Sanchi, Bhopal, which was then a great Buddhist university. The shrine is within the railed enclosure at the top.

BUDDHISM began as a form of Hinduism. It was begun by Siddhartha Gautama, the Buddha or Enlightened, who lived from about 560 to 480 BC. He was a rich and powerful prince by birth, but he gave up all his wealth and power to become a wandering beggar. The religion which he founded has spread far and has taken different forms, so it is hardly possible in a few words to give more than a very rough picture of it.

Buddha did not accept the caste system, though he did believe in reincarnation and Nirvana. He said that all men, whatever their class or nation, could strive towards perfection, and he taught simple practical rules to help them.

First, he said, people must understand that pain is caused by desire, selfishness, and they must see the need to overcome this.

In order to improve, they must follow the Noble Eightfold Path: Right Belief, Right Purpose, Right Speech, Right Behaviour, Right Livelihood, Right Effort, Right Contemplation, Right Concentration.

They must avoid the five great faults: killing, stealing, lying, adultery and drunkenness.

These teachings were simple and practical, and quickly spread. For centuries there were many millions of Buddhists in India, but eventually Hinduism revived and displaced it. Meanwhile, Buddhism became the most important religion in other eastern countries, like Tibet, Indo-China, China and Japan.

The elephant gate of the palace at Gwalior, built about 1500.

Indian books were often beautifully decorated and illustrated. The upper picture shows a legendary battle between Scythians (on the right, dressed as Muslims) and Jains (followers of a religion rather like Buddhism and founded at about the same time). The 'sun' in the middle of the text is the string hole ornament. Strings had been necessary when books were made of palm leaves, and although books were now made of paper the writers went on decorating where the hole would have been. The lower picture shows the parable of the ram. A calf was jealous of the much better fed ram until he realised that it was being fattened for slaughter (shown in the middle row). Both manuscripts were made about the middle of the fifteenth century.

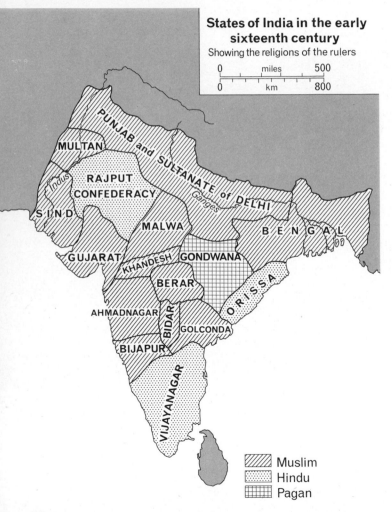

States of India in the early sixteenth century

Showing the religions of the rulers

| 0 | miles | 500 |
| 0 | km | 800 |

PUNJAB and SULTANATE of DELHI
MULTAN
RAJPUT
CONFEDERACY
Indus
Ganges
SIND
MALWA
BENGAL
GUJARAT
KHANDESH
GONDWANA
BERAR
ORISSA
AHMADNAGAR
BIDAR
GOLCONDA
BIJAPUR
VIJAYANAGAR

Muslim
Hindu
Pagan

THE RULERS OF INDIA. Though most of the teeming millions of Indians in 1498 were Hindus, many of the kingdoms were ruled by Muslims. Since the tenth century AD waves of Muslim warriors had at various times surged into India from the north-west, and formed kingdoms for themselves in northern India – the Punjab and the Ganges Valley, especially. These Muslim kings and their followers seem usually to have remained as a separate class of rulers in their own kingdoms, while their subjects remained Hindus. The kings of India, Muslim and Hindu alike, spent much of their energies fighting one another, and trying to take one another's kingdoms.

To most of these kings and the people they ruled, the arrival of the Portuguese on a few parts of the coast must have made very little difference. The Indians had their own business to attend to; the Portuguese were only touching the fringes of a great civilisation. You may have guessed, from the few photographs on pages 34–7, that such work could only be produced by the artists and craftsmen of a rich and strong civilisation. This is how Vijayanagar, the capital of the Hindu Empire in southern India, seemed to a Portuguese who visited it early in the sixteenth century.

'The size of this city I do not write here, because it cannot all be seen from any one spot, but I climbed a hill whence I could see a great part of it; I could not see it all because it lies between several ranges of hills. What I saw from thence seemed to me as large as Rome, and very beautiful to the sight; there are many groves of trees within it, in the gardens of the houses, and many conduits of water which flow into the midst of it, and in many places there are artificial lakes . . . The people in this city are countless in number, so much so that I do not wish to write it down for fear it should be thought fabulous.'

Building an empire

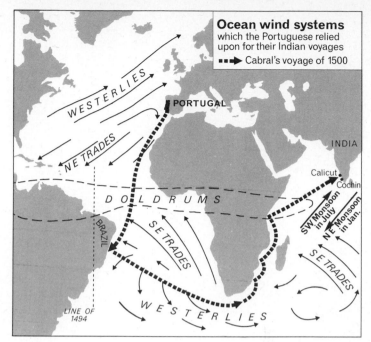

Ocean wind systems which the Portuguese relied upon for their Indian voyages
■■■▶ Cabral's voyage of 1500

WESTERLIES

PORTUGAL

NE TRADES

INDIA

Calicut
Cochin

DOLDRUMS

BRAZIL

SE TRADES

SW Monsoon in July
NE Monsoon in Jan.

SE TRADES

LINE OF 1494

WESTERLIES

Chips of brazil wood, actual size. The dark reddish wood was broken like this or ground into powder, and then boiled to produce a strong red dye.

The strategy

The Portuguese government lost no time in following up the work of Vasco da Gama. In 1500 Pedro Alvares Cabral sailed with a fleet of thirteen ships. On the way he went so far out into the Atlantic, to take advantage of the strong, steady Trade Winds, that he came upon the eastern tip of South America, which was on the Portuguese side of the dividing line of 1494. In the years after this discovery, a small number of Portuguese settlers went there in order to cut down and sell the brazil wood, which was valued in dyeing. The country was to take its name from the dye-wood.

Cabral's fleet, and the others which followed, were strong enough to fight and defeat the Arab ships which opposed them. Because they were mainly trying to take over the trade of the eastern seas, this was the most important thing to be sure of. But even the stoutest ships needed bases, and also the Portuguese had to have some ports where they could be certain of being able to collect their cargoes. Safe harbours at strategic points were needed, and the next map shows what the Portuguese did, and how quickly they did it.

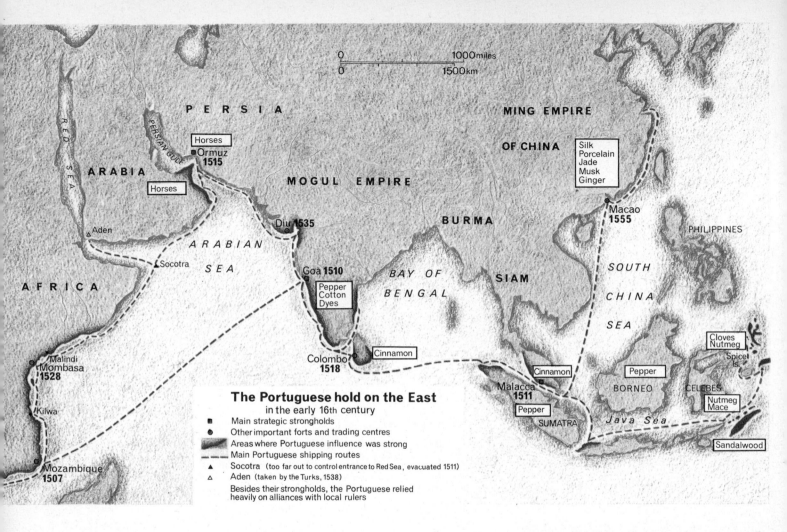

The Portuguese hold on the East
in the early 16th century
■ Main strategic strongholds
● Other important forts and trading centres
▨ Areas where Portuguese influence was strong
▬ ▬ Main Portuguese shipping routes
▲ Socotra (too far out to control entrance to Red Sea, evacuated 1511)
△ Aden (taken by the Turks, 1538)
Besides their strongholds, the Portuguese relied heavily on alliances with local rulers

Notice that they were doing two things. They were taking positions which protected their routes from the Spice Islands, in the East Indies, and India itself, round Africa. They were also blocking, against the Arab traders, the straits which led into the Red Sea and the Persian Gulf, and so towards the old markets of Egypt and Syria.

One man especially, Afonso de Albuquerque, who was Viceroy of the Indies from 1509 to 1515, is regarded as the creator of the Portuguese Empire in the East, and you can find out from the map which strategic places were taken in his time. Though he was very important, the empire was not the work of any one man. It was not a land empire. The Portuguese kings and their governments were interested in collecting the rich trade of the East. They were not anxious to rule over other lands and nations, though they would capture whatever was necessary to help their trade, and they also wished to help Christian missionaries to spread their religion. It was only because they limited their ambitions like this that the Portuguese were able to build so quickly an empire covering such an enormous part of the world's surface. Even allowing for the limits, it was an astonishing feat, especially in so short a time. How did they manage it?

Portuguese carracks off a rocky coast, painted probably by Cornelis Antoniszoon about 1530. These represent the biggest type of ship, able to carry bulky cargo and heavy armament.

below right:
A modern attempt to show how the guns could have been arranged near the stern of the English warship *Henry Grâce à Dieu*, the highest part of an unusually large and heavily armed ship. The diagram shows the variety of guns which could be used, and how they could be mounted.

below:
Early sixteenth-century breech-loading swivel gun, called a *columbrina*; length $58\frac{1}{4}$ in (148 cm), calibre $3\frac{1}{8}$ in (8 cm). The breech piece has been removed and is lying beside the handle; it was possible to have spares ready loaded when rapid fire was needed.

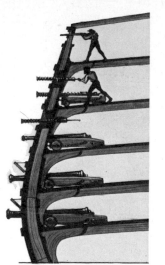

The methods

We have already seen two of the main reasons for the Portuguese success. They planned and prepared carefully whenever they could, and they had the intelligence to pick positions of first-rate strategic value. But these positions could not be taken without fighting. At times the Portuguese acted as the friends of one Indian ruler against another, and gained a stronghold either as a reward or as part of the loot. At other times they attacked Muslim ports in the name of Christianity. Whatever excuses they had, though, and whatever allies, their successes really depended on their armed strength.

At sea, it seems that much of their success was because they had stronger ships than their Arab and Indian opponents, ships which had been built to stand up to the long voyage round Africa and designed to carry guns. Though we know much less about Arab and Indian ships of the early sixteenth century than we do about European, it seems fairly certain that they were not suitable for firing guns, and not so capable of withstanding the shot from enemy guns.

41

Portuguese soldiers of about 1500, a drawing based upon pictures, armour and weapons of that time. Some officers may have worn full armour. Most soldiers were more lightly armoured. Strong jackets with small iron plates riveted into them were popular, and helmets of various types which gave good protection without completely covering the face.

On land, or in hand-to-hand fighting at sea, the Portuguese had other technical advantages. Though clumsy in some ways, the crossbows and the matchlock hand-guns of the Portuguese were hard-hitting weapons. It is likely, too, that many of the warriors who fought the Portuguese did not have armour of anything like the efficiency of that which was used in Europe.

(This technical superiority, especially in weapons, is something that you will notice time after time in the story of how different nations built empires all over world.)

Of course, the Portuguese had to be able to use their weapons, and they showed themselves on many occasions to be able soldiers. In their very first war in India the Portuguese, seventy-one men in three ships, victoriously defended a ford against the entire forces of Calicut, 75,000 men and 160 ships and boats. We may suspect that the figures are grossly exaggerated, that many of the enemy army were servants, not fighters, that the struggle did not go on very furiously for most of the five months it is supposed to have lasted. Nevertheless, the Portuguese won many victories against heavy odds, and clearly felt confident of their own superiority.

The cathedral at Goa, begun in 1562. Spacious and dignified in the Renaissance style of architecture, it helps us to understand why visitors to Goa were impressed by the city's stately buildings. The missing tower was destroyed in a storm in 1766.

In such ways a comparatively small number of Portuguese took and held a wide empire, thousands of miles across the seas from home. It may have been the knowledge of how few they were which caused some of them to be deliberately cruel. On his second voyage Vasco da Gama hanged thirty-eight fishermen of Calicut simply as a warning to their ruler; he had the corpses thrown overboard to drift to the city, but first had the heads, hands and feet cut off, piled into a boat, and also set to drift ashore with a message to the king. At Ormuz Albuquerque mutilated the people when he took the town, and at Goa he perpetrated a general massacre. It was a deliberate policy of terror. Whether or not it helped by making people unwilling to resist the Portuguese is difficult to say. It certainly won them few friends.

Some of the Portuguese did the reputation of their nation a great deal of harm by becoming pirates. Their robberies and murders, like the ruthlessness of many of the Portuguese governors, cannot have given the peoples of the East a very good opinion of the civilisation of the West.

Against this background, missionaries tried to spread Christianity. The Portuguese soldiers in the early years often believed that they were fighting for the true faith against infidels – this belief that God was on their side may have helped them to win victories – and great churches were built in the towns which they ruled. Beyond, although saintly men like Francis Xavier spent their lives preaching it, the religion from the West won over comparatively few converts.

The decline of the empire

The Portuguese were the first of the European nations to explore the oceans, and the first to make for themselves an overseas empire. Other nations were to follow their example. So it is important to understand as much as we can about them and what they achieved.

We have seen why and how they built their empire. Soon, though, their grasp began to weaken. Why? It seemed as though they had made a tremendous effort, and could not keep it up. Usually it is very misleading to talk about a country or a nation as if it were a person, but this time there may be some truth in the idea. Portugal was small. Thousands of men sailed east, and probably only a few ever returned. How long could Portugal go on finding enough men who were both willing and able to hold the empire, especially as difficulties began to pile up? It must have been a strain.

Of course, many jobs could be done by men who had been born in the East, the sons of Portuguese who had married Indian women. But in many empires and at many times people of mixed race have been in an awkward position. They have often been made to feel that they were not really respected by either their father's people or their mother's. Though the Portuguese sometimes gave important posts to men of mixed race, we can understand that such men may sometimes have had too little confidence to be able to deal firmly with proud Portuguese captains and Indian noblemen.

Whether or not Portugal failed to find enough of the right sort of men to keep her empire going is a question about which historians can argue, for there can be no real proof. There is no argument, however, about the way Portugal's misfortunes increased. In 1580 King Philip II of Spain inherited the throne of Portugal. This led to Portugal's becoming involved in King Philip's wars with the Dutch and the English

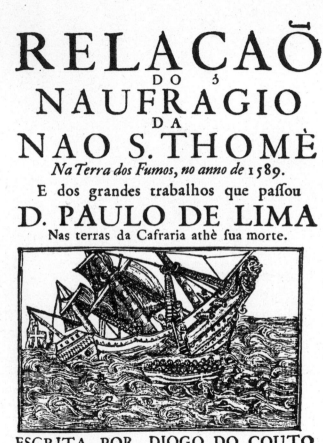

RELAÇAÕ
DO
NAUFRAGIO
DA
NAO S. THOMÈ
Na Terra dos Fumos, no anno de 1589.
E dos grandes trabalhos que paſſou
D. PAULO DE LIMA
Nas terras da Cafraria athè ſua morte.

ESCRITA POR DIOGO DO COUTO
Guarda mòr da Torre do Tombo.

A rogo da Senhora D. Anna de Lima irmãa do dito D. Paulo de Lima no Anno de 1611.
Tom. II.   V

In the eighteenth century a collection of accounts of Portuguese shipwrecks was published. It was called *The Tragic History of the Sea*, and this is a good example. Translated, the title reads: *Narrative of the shipwreck of the great ship 'Sao Thome' in the Land of the Fumos, in the year 1589 and of the toil and tribulation undergone by Dom Paulo de Lima in the regions of Kaffraria until his death.*

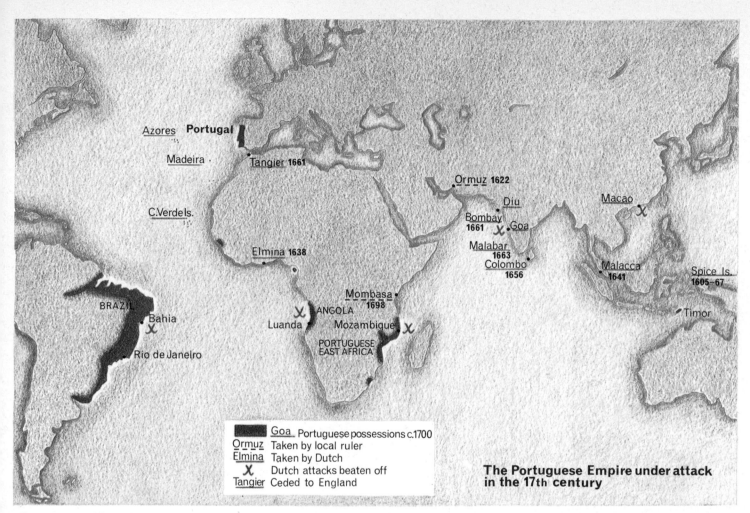

Azores • **Portugal**

Madeira •

Tangier **1661**

C.Verde Is.

Elmina **1638**

BRAZIL

Bahia

Rio de Janeiro

Luanda ANGOLA

Mombasa **1698**

Mozambique

PORTUGUESE
EAST AFRICA

Ormuz **1622**

Diu

Bombay **1661** Goa

Malabar **1663**

Colombo **1656**

Macao

Malacca **1641**

Spice Is. **1605–67**

Timor

	Goa Portuguese possessions c.1700
Ormuz	Taken by local ruler
Elmina	Taken by Dutch
X	Dutch attacks beaten off
Tangier	Ceded to England

**The Portuguese Empire under attack
in the 17th century**

who, as you will read later in this book, set about taking some of the eastern trade for themselves, building their own forts and trading posts and attacking those of the Portuguese.

Meanwhile there were trading difficulties in Europe. The chief market for Portuguese trade had been Antwerp, in the Netherlands; Antwerp suffered badly from wars, and became a poorer trading centre, while Dutch and English ports became richer. Foreign bankers became less ready to help Portuguese trade by lending money.

There were terrible losses at sea, too. Some ships were taken by the English or Dutch, but the worst losses were by shipwreck, often on the coast of South Africa, when the big ships,

overloaded with cargo and passengers, were sailing home from the Indies. Between 1550 and 1650 these losses averaged more than one great ship per year.

In 1640 the Portuguese rose against Spain. They had to struggle through a long and exhausting war before Portugal was once again an independent country.

Despite all her difficulties and enemies, Portugal managed to hang on to a very large part of her empire. Other European countries, however, went ahead and built up bigger empires and collected more wealth from trade with the East. Portugal was never able to regain the lead which she had held in the early sixteenth century.

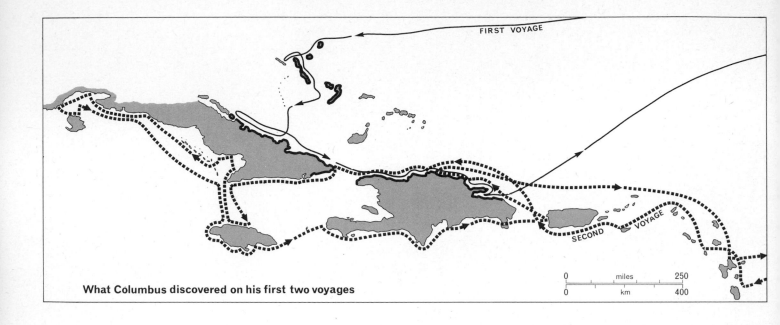

FIRST VOYAGE

SECOND VOYAGE

| 0 | miles | 250 |
| 0 | km | 400 |

What Columbus discovered on his first two voyages

The first voyage

When the proposals of Christopher Columbus were rejected by the king of Portugal, as you read on page 31, he had better luck in Spain, and found land on the far side of the Atlantic. This map shows you the coasts he discovered, on his first voyage in 1492, and how it was impossible for him to know, from what he saw, how far the land might extend. All the same, he was confident that he had reached the Far East. Here were the Indies, he asserted.

It was rather disappointing that the people there, the Indians as he naturally called them, were not in the least like the civilised Orientals whom he had expected to find. They were friendly and helpful, but primitive. So far from wearing silks, living in huge cities, trading in spices and jewels; they wore no clothes at all, sheltered in crude huts, and lived on the plants and animals which they found near them. But, of course,

this could easily be explained; this was doubtless only a remote part of the vast empire of some eastern monarch – the emperor of China, say – and the civilised parts were still hundreds of miles away. Even these simple Indians had a little gold, tiny pieces which they used as ornaments on their noses. They did not seem to value it highly, and gladly gave it to the Spaniards in exchange for such toys as mirrors, red caps and the tinkling bells which were used in Europe to decorate hawks' hoods. Also, they indicated to Columbus that there was more gold in the distant mountains, and that a great king lived there, far away.

Columbus returned to Spain, sure that he had found a quick route to the treasures of the East. Everyone believed the same. On his next voyage, in the autumn of 1493, he had seventeen ships and about 1200 men, all of them expecting that they would soon become rich in the Indies.

They were bitterly disappointed. The first shock was when they discovered islands inhabited by the savage Caribs, the people who have given their name to the Caribbean Sea, and the word 'cannibal' to our language. Then the fleet reached Hispaniola to find that the small party of men whom Columbus had left behind on his first voyage had all been killed. (They had probably deserved it, by their ill-treatment of the Indians, so Columbus did not take revenge.) A settlement was made

below left: Of all the peoples who dwelt in the West Indies in 1492, only a few Caribs survive. This photograph of one of them, standing before his house and holding an example of his work, was taken in 1970 in Dominica.

below right: The attempt of a European artist to depict Spaniards approaching the people of Hispaniola. It is an illustration in a 1493 edition of a letter from Columbus. The artist failed to get the ship right: he merely used an existing picture of a Venetian war-galley!

in what later turned out to be a very unhealthy place. The food brought from Spain was soon used up, and the settlers found that native food did not suit them. They would probably have put up with it all if they had been getting rich, but they soon realised that this was not to be so easy. They blamed Columbus for having deceived them, which was not entirely fair; and they turned their anger against the Indians, which was completely unfair.

Death of a nation

The one thing that all the Spaniards craved was gold. Columbus was as eager as anybody. He had insisted on great rewards for his discovery – Admiral of the Ocean Sea, Governor of the lands he had found, the title of Don, as well as a share in the profits – and all would be lost if his discovery should prove valueless. So the Indians, helpless against European weapons, were forced to collect gold dust; every Indian over the age of fourteen had to bring in a hawk's bell full, every three months. There was not enough gold dust to go round, but this did not save the Indians from cruel punishment if they failed. Also, they were expected to feed the Spaniards and work for them. They had never learnt to work more than was necessary to grow the exact amount of food that they wanted to eat themselves. They simply did not understand how to work regularly to produce more than they needed. The Spaniards thought them lazy, or deliberately awkward, or so stupid that there was serious doubt about whether they were human beings at all; their only policy was stern punishment. (Nobody bothered to recall that Queen Isabella had given orders that the Indians were to be well treated, and must not be enslaved.)

Miserable and hopeless, the Indians began to die in their thousands. Some, in desperation, tried to fight; they were massacred, hunted down with fierce dogs. Some of the Spaniards were said to be so callous as to cut down unoffending Indians for no better reason than to test the edge of their swords.

Eventually these horrors stopped. The missionary friars and the officials sent out from Spain began to stand between the surviving Indians and the settlers, and Negro slaves were brought from Africa to do the work which was too hard for the Indians. But by then it was too late. In Hispaniola, or Cuba, or Jamaica you will find today none of the descendants

A modern West Indian in Barbados, grafting grapefruit. Like most West Indians, he is a descendant of the Africans brought across the Atlantic as slave labour.

of those Indians. The pathetic remnant who survived the massacres died out. A whole people had been exterminated.

This horrible tale has often been used against the Spaniards by their enemies, and it truly brands those early settlers as greedy, cruel murderers. But it is only fair to remember that we should not even know of those crimes if it had not been for Spaniards like Bishop Las Casas, who roused the Spanish government to try to control the settlers. Also, most other European nations were guilty of equal cruelties, and worse, when their turn came to build empires beyond the seas.

A new continent, a new ocean

Balboa crosses the isthmus

Every year more adventurers sailed west from Spain. Though the West Indies had not yet produced much treasure, there was always hope. For instance, Columbus on his third voyage had discovered pearl fisheries. More islands were discovered, and a great mainland mass began to take shape. If you look at the names and dates on the map, you will be able to work out the order in which, bit by bit, men came to realise that a great continent lay near the islands. Most of the explorers sailed under the flag of Spain, though to the north there were a few from England, while Portugal was keeping an eye on anything to the east of the line of 1494.

The great question was: Is this mainland part of Asia? To his dying day Columbus said that it was, but more and more people became convinced that it was not. One of the early explorers was an Italian, Amerigo Vespucci, and his name was used for part of the mainland he had discovered – America. This was not Asia, but a New World.

Unfortunately, the New World had not so far produced anything to equal the riches of the Far East, to which it was barring the way. How big a barrier was it? Was there a way through it, or round it?

It was sheer luck that the first Spanish settlements on the mainland happened to be where the mainland was narrowest. Among the bold captains who, from the unhealthy shanty town in Darien, risked death from disease or poisoned arrows on their quests through the jungle there was Vasco Nuñez de Balboa. He, unlike others, made friends with some Indian tribes, and was told of a great sea which lay to the south. He followed their directions, and he found it. As far as he could tell, it was a vast ocean, and it stretched southwards. Therefore he called it the South Sea.

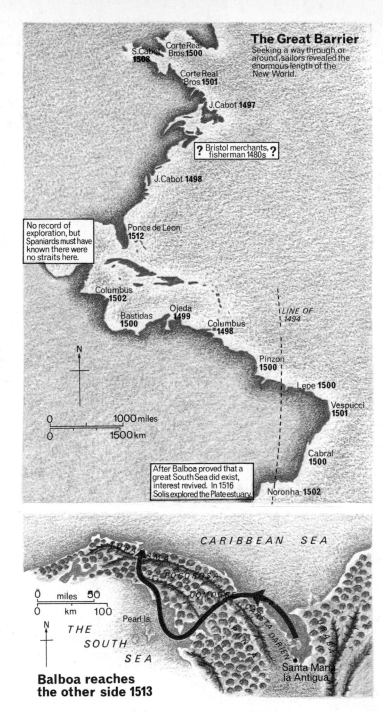

The Great Barrier
Seeking a way through or around, sailors revealed the enormous length of the New World.

S. Cabot 1508
Corte Real Bros. 1500
Corte Real Bros. 1501
J. Cabot 1497
? Bristol merchants, fisherman 1480s ?
J. Cabot 1498
No record of exploration, but Spaniards must have known there were no straits here.
Ponce de Leon 1512
Columbus 1502
Bastidas 1500
Ojeda 1499
Columbus 1498
LINE OF 1494
N
0 1000 miles
0 1500 km
Pinzon 1500
Lepe 1500
Vespucci 1501
Cabral 1500
After Balboa proved that a great South Sea did exist, interest revived. In 1516 Solis explored the Plate estuary.
Noronha 1502

CARIBBEAN SEA
CUBAGANA
POCOROSA
COMOGR
CARETA DARIEN
PONCA
URABA
0 miles 50
0 km 100
Pearl Is.
THE SOUTH SEA
N
Santa Maria la Antigua

Balboa reaches the other side 1513

The Straits of Magellan

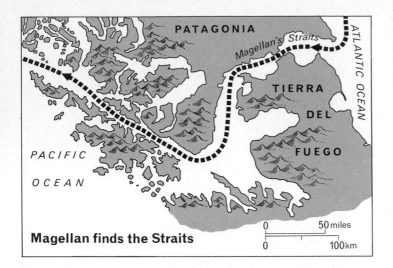

PATAGONIA

Magellan's Straits

ATLANTIC OCEAN

TIERRA DEL FUEGO

PACIFIC OCEAN

0   50 miles
0   100 km

Magellan finds the Straits

below left: The rocky shores of the Magellan Strait.
right: One of the many inlets off the Strait.

The sea was there, but how could ships reach it, in order to sail across to Asia? Explorers felt their way along the coast, southwards. From time to time they came to wide inlets which raised their hopes that they had found straits cutting through the continent, but it always turned out that these were only great bays or huge river mouths – signs that the continent itself was enormous.

The man who finally found a way through was a Portuguese who had served in the East Indies and against the Muslims of North Africa. His name was Fernao de Magalhaes, or Ferdinand Magellan as it is usually written in English. The king of Portugal had not rewarded him as well as he wanted, so Magellan went to Spain and offered to lead a Spanish expedition to the Spice Islands. In August 1519 he sailed from Seville with five ships and about 280 men. Fourteen months later, after wintering on the barren coast of Patagonia and stamping out a mutiny among his officers, he discovered the twisting, forbidding, dangerous channel which is now called Magellan's Straits. On 28 November 1520, with the three ships which remained to him, he entered the South Sea. After the constant dangers from squalls and rocks, he thankfully

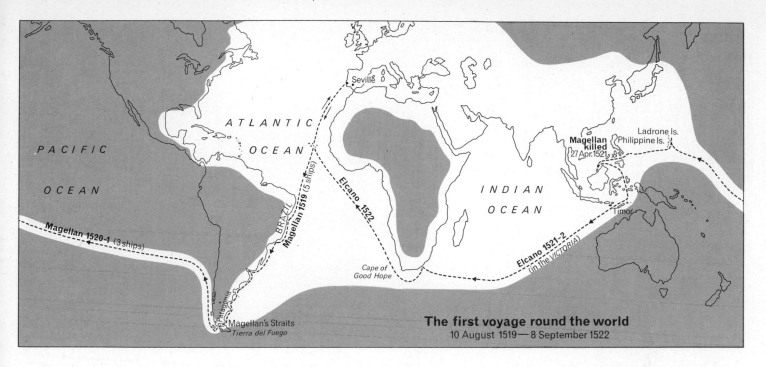

The first voyage round the world
10 August 1519 — 8 September 1522

called this great expanse of water, where the winds blew steadily, the Pacific.

The vast size of the Pacific was what nobody had fully understood. Before Magellan reached the islands off the coast of Asia, his men were dying of starvation; by pure bad luck they had not sighted any land where they could find food. On one of the islands later to be called the Philippines, after Philip II of Spain, Magellan was killed helping one of the local kings in a war against another.

The remaining officers now had to think about how to get back to Spain. They were on the edge of the Spice Islands, and the Portuguese would have a short way with any strange ships and sailors they caught in the seas which they claimed by the treaty of 1494. This made it dangerous to try to sail home by way of the Indian Ocean and round Africa. Yet the risk of trying to sail back the way they had come seemed even greater. Captain Juan Sebastian de Elcano decided for the voyage round Africa. On Monday, 8 September 1522 the battered ship *Victoria* with eighteen men aboard came home to Seville. They were all that was left of Magellan's expedition. They were the first men to have travelled round the world.

Despite her great achievement, it seems that nobody bothered to preserve a picture of the *Victoria*. This, the earliest picture we have, is merely what a Renaissance artist invented to decorate a map.

The great conquests: Central America

The Aztecs of Mexico

An Aztec market, as imagined by Diego Rivera, a modern Mexican artist. In the background is a view of Tenochtitlan itself.

The Magellan-Elcano voyage had been a splendid feat, but it had shown that the westward sea route to the Far East was too long. Just as this road to riches was closed, however, there appeared new, almost unbelievable, opportunities in the New World itself.

You may have noticed on the map on page 49 that the early explorers of the American coast were more interested in searching southwards or northwards, and it was not until 1518 that the Spaniards living in Cuba came to think that there was something interesting due west. An expedition was sent to explore Yucatan, which came back with reports that the Indians there were rich. Next year an expedition left Cuba to seek those riches. It was commanded by Hernan Cortes, and was between 500 and 600 strong.

With this force Cortes began the conquest of a great civilisation which was ruled by a powerful, warlike nation – the Aztecs. The story of how he did it is one of the most exciting in history – perhaps the most exciting of all – and it needs much more detail than we have space for here. It is better not to spoil the story by trying to tell it in a page or two; you must read it in another book. But it is necessary here to explain something about the Aztecs, about their greatness and the flaws in it.

Mexico City, or Tenochtitlan as it was called, stood in the midst of a wide lake in a great valley. The islands on which it was built were largely artificial, and the vegetable and flower gardens were rafts of basketwork and earth. The causeways linking the city to the shores of the lake were broken by gaps with removable bridges, partly for defence but also to allow freer movement to the canoes which swarmed upon the lake. Along one of the causeways ran an aqueduct to supply the city with fresh water. The city was large, almost certainly larger than any city in Europe; it probably had not less than 250,000 inhabitants, and one early estimate is as high as a million. It was as beautiful as it was large, with its canals and streets and squares lined by white houses, palaces and temples, the people clad in brightly patterned loincloths and cloaks, the nobles resplendent in garments woven with brilliant feathers. The city was full, bustling. The markets were thronged, people buying and selling articles of all sorts but keeping everything orderly and clean.

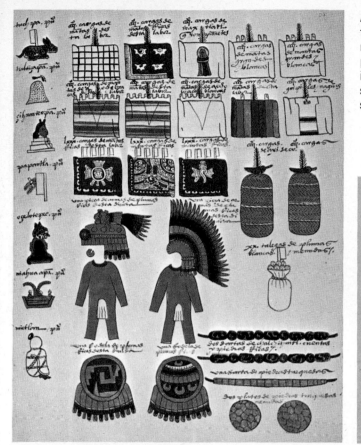

left: Part of an Aztec annual tribute list, a copy made for the first Spanish viceroy. Down the left side are symbols representing the towns owing the tribute, and the other pictures represent the articles owed as tribute. They include cloaks, padded war-suits with crested helmets, shields, beads and pendants of jade and turquoise, and sacks of raw materials.

above: Aztec featherwork was uniquely brilliant, but only a little remains. The so-called Crown of Montezuma, made of quetzal plumes, is probably the head-dress of a high priest. It was presented by Montezuma to Cortes, who sent it to Charles V.

The double-headed serpent is $17\frac{1}{8}$ in (43 cm) long and is made of turquoise mosaic fixed on wood. The eyes were probably polished circles of shell and iron pyrites. It could be worn across the chest, with a head projecting at each of the wearer's shoulders.

A number of Cortes' men later wrote accounts of their great adventure, and they tell us of how the Spaniards were struck by admiration and awe when they beheld Mexico. One of them, Bernal Diaz del Castillo, writing in his old age of what he had seen as a young soldier, has often been quoted: 'We were amazed, and said that it was like the enchantments they tell of in the legend of Amadis . . . and some of our soldiers even asked whether the things that we saw were not a dream . . . I say again that I stood looking at it and thought that never in the world would there be discovered other lands such as these, for at that time there was no Peru, nor any thought of it. Of all these wonders that I then beheld, today all is overthrown and lost, nothing left standing.'

The whole valley of Mexico was full of cities and teemed with people. It was a prosperous and pleasant land. The people themselves delighted in flowers, in songs and poems. They were governed by strict laws, but it seems that the respect for law was so great that there was little crime. Everyone knew his place in society – priest, warrior, merchant and peasant – and most people stayed in their own class, though it was possible to move and nobles and merchants were sometimes discontented or ambitious. Slavery existed, but it seems to have been comparatively mild, for the slaves had their own rights, and their children were free.

But there was a terrible and horrible side to Aztec life. They believed in what was probably the most hideous religion that has ever been practised by a civilised people. The first of these pictures shows one of the most beautifully made objects in the British Museum, carved and polished from rock crystal. What was the outlook of people who spent such care on such a thing? Next you see a picture of the chief god of Mexico. Compare this with the statues of Greek and Roman gods, of Christ and the Christian saints, of the Hindu gods and of Buddha. The final picture shows the type of knife used to sacrifice human beings. The victim was stretched over a stone while a priest slashed him open with the razor-sharp obsidian blade and tore out the living heart. In Mexico City alone many thousands died like this each year, on the altars at the top of the pyramid-like temples. Their skulls were stacked in a gigantic rack. Most of the victims were prisoners of war, but many were Aztecs themselves, for it was no disgrace to be sacrificed. The Aztecs believed, indeed, that sacrificial victims were sure of a pleasant life after death, which was more

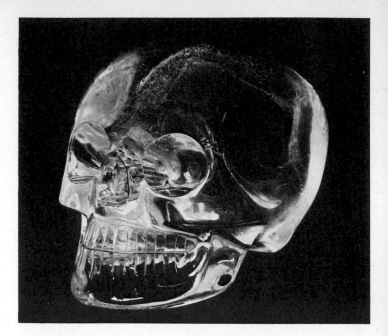

Skull of rock crystal, $5\frac{11}{16}$ in (15 cm) high.

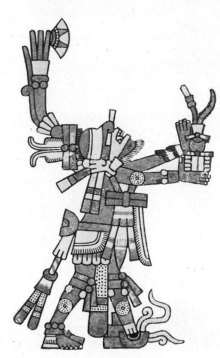

left: Huitzilopochtli, from an Aztec manuscript. He wears on his head a warrior's plume, and over his heart a priest's sacrificial knife. His left foot is replaced by a smoking mirror, because he sacrificed it in making the earth.

than most people could expect.

It was not that the Aztecs enjoyed bloodshed for its own sake, as the Assyrians and Romans often seem to have done. They believed that the sun needed a constant supply of human blood, or else it would die and the whole world would die with it. Because of this, in their battles they were often more anxious to take prisoners than to kill or chase their enemies. They kept on a continual war with the city of Tlaxcala, which they could have wiped out if they had wished, so that they could always get a supply of prisoners.

This religion horrified the Spaniards. Yet it has been argued that it is not fair to blame the Aztecs too much for the blood they shed, because they had been brought up to believe it was right. On the other side, the Spaniards believed in Christianity, yet they were often cruel killers. The Spaniards wiped out the evil religion of the Aztecs and brought Christianity. Who deserves praise or blame, Aztecs or Spaniards or both?

When they fought against Cortes the Aztecs placed on their skull racks not only Spanish heads (identifiable by their beards) but also the heads of the strange and terrible beasts which the Spaniards rode. The drawing above is by an Indian artist several years after the conquest.

below: Sacrificial knife, overall length 12½ in (32 cm), with chalcedony blade. The handle is of wood inlaid with shell, turquoise and malachite. It represents a crouching 'Eagle Knight', one of a select band of warriors who had earned their distinctive uniform and eagle-head helmets by capturing prisoners of war for sacrifice.

In one way the Aztec religion helped Cortes. It had been predicted that Quetzalcoatl would soon return. Quetzalcoatl was a fair-skinned god who disliked human sacrifice and had been driven away, across the Eastern Sea, by the other gods. When Cortes appeared with wonderful ships and weapons, it was natural that the Aztec ruler, Montezuma, should believe that this had something to do with the prophecy. While he hesitated, Cortes advanced.

Another weakness of the Aztec Empire was that it was not really an empire at all. The Aztecs and their allies lived in only three cities, Tenochtitlan itself, Texcoco and Tacuba. Most of the other peoples of central Mexico had been civilised for many centuries before the Aztecs had arrived from the north, in the early fourteenth century, and had bitterly resented the rise to power of these bloodthirsty newcomers. When the Aztecs became very powerful, in the earlier part of the fifteenth century, they did not try to rule completely over the places they conquered. They usually allowed these other cities to keep their own lords and customs as long as they did nothing against the Aztecs and provided a regular tribute. Many of these cities, when they saw that Cortes was strong, took the chance to help him against the Aztecs.

Finally, despite all their wonderful works, the Aztecs were backward in some practical matters. They had neither wheels nor beasts of burden, and goods had to be carried by human porters. Horses, especially war-horses, astonished and terrified them at first. Also, they lacked iron. The Spaniards owed some of their success in battle to their guns, but they had few of these and they sometimes lacked gunpowder. Their steel blades, with the horses, were the weapons which brought victory. Aztec warriors carried the *macuahuitl*, a heavy wooden sword edged with obsidian; it was a deadly weapon, but not against iron armour. Aztec armour, of padded cotton and wood, was good protection against their own weapons, but could not stop the thrust of a steel point.

Though they fought heroically, and nearly overwhelmed the Spaniards, the Aztecs were finally beaten. They defended Tenochtitlan so bravely that the Spaniards had to destroy it, street by street, before the survivors surrendered on 13 August 1521, and Cortes was master of Mexico.

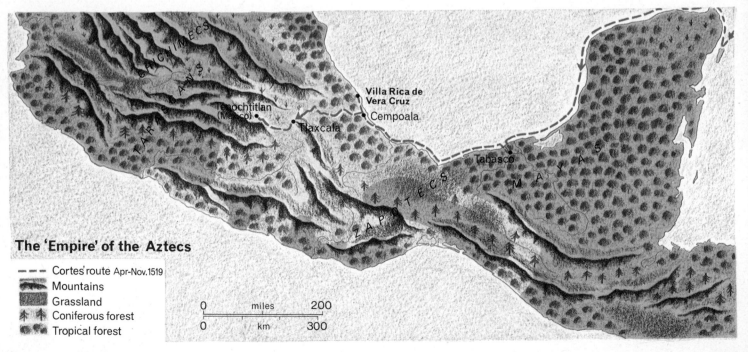

The 'Empire' of the Aztecs

- - - Cortes' route Apr-Nov. 1519
Mountains
Grassland
Coniferous forest
Tropical forest

0   miles   200
0   km   300

DIAGRAM OF TENOCHTITLAN

and its surroundings, printed at Nuremberg in 1523 and supposedly based on a sketch by Cortes himself. It is badly out of scale, but it does give a vivid impression of the position of the most important features as they appeared to the Spaniards.

Key:

1 Southern causeway to Ixtapalapa, the road by which the Spaniards first came to the city

2 Western causeway to Tacuba

3 Northern causeway to Tepeyacac

4 Port for canoes plying to Texcoco

5 Dykes for protection against floods

6 Aqueduct carrying main water supply from the springs of Chapultepec

7 Main square of Tenochtitlan

8 Main square of Tlatelolco, the northern half of the city

9 Sacred enclosure, with temples, skull racks and an idol (shown without a head)

10 Montezuma's palace

11 Montezuma's garden

12 Montezuma's menagerie

13 Montezuma's pleasure-gardens outside the city

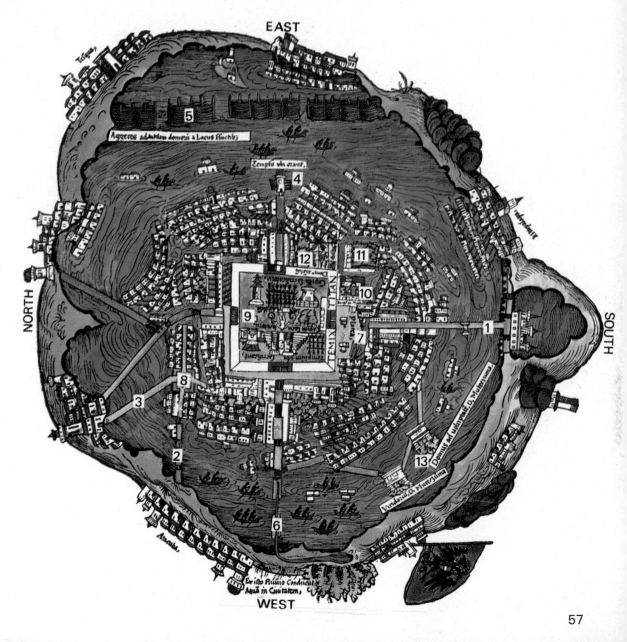

The Spanish Conquest
of Central America

[Map labels: Merida 1542, Campeche 1540, MAYAS, OLID, CORTÉS, Santiago de Guatemala (Antigua) 1524, Trujillo 1525, ALVARADO, San Salvador 1528, GUATEMALA, Leon 1523, CORDOBA, Granada 1522, CARIBBEAN SEA, GIL GONZALEZ DAVILA, Panama 1519, PEDRARIAS DAVILA, S Maria la Antigua 1510, miles 0 300, km 0 500]

New Spain

The conquered land was named New Spain, and the problems of governing it were more difficult, if less exciting, than those of taking it. We shall think about these problems later, but now it is better to finish the story of the conquests.

Many of Cortes' men, and those who came afterwards led expeditions out from central Mexico. Some marched south, overcoming the civilised Mayas and the other tribes of the southern jungles, until they met other Spaniards moving northwards from Darien and Panama.

To the north of Mexico, many Spaniards were lured onwards by legends of the Seven Cities of Cibola, civilised and full of gold. Moving due north from Mexico itself, they found California, the Rocky Mountains and Grand Canyon, and the prairies of North America. Others started from the islands and explored Florida and the lands around the Mississippi. They came upon many Indian nations, from the nomadic hunters of the prairies (whose lives were later to be changed when they learned to use the horses which the Spaniards had brought and which ran wild on the great plains) to the pueblo people, who dwelt in villages which really did look like cities when first seen from afar. But none of these explorers found the riches they were seeking. The next great prize lay in the opposite direction, south from Panama.

left: The mighty architecture of the Maya civilisation had long been overgrown and forgotten when in the 1840s it was revealed by the drawings of Frederick Catherwood. This one shows part of the ruins of Uxmal, Yucatan.

opposite from left to right:
The Grand Canyon of the Colorado.
The arid southern plains of Arizona.
The Florida swamps.

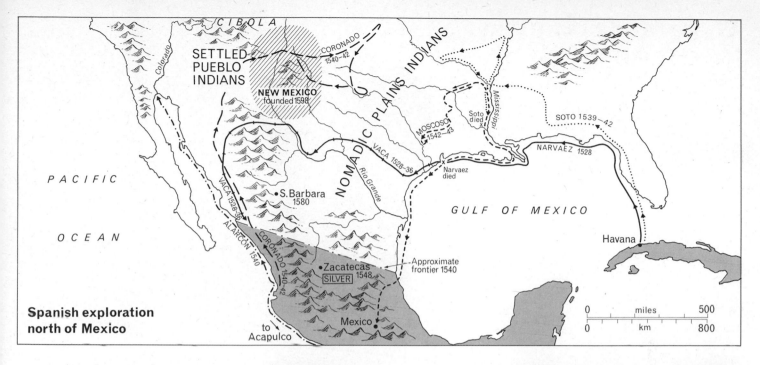

Spanish exploration north of Mexico

Map labels:
- CIBOLA
- SETTLED PUEBLO INDIANS
- NEW MEXICO founded 1598
- CORONADO 1540-42
- NOMADIC PLAINS INDIANS
- Colorado
- PACIFIC OCEAN
- VACA 1528-36
- VACA 1528-36
- ALARCÓN 1540
- CORONADO 1540-42
- S. Barbara 1580
- Rio Grande
- MOSCOSO 1542-43
- Soto died
- Mississippi
- SOTO 1539-42
- NARVAEZ 1528
- Narvaez died
- GULF OF MEXICO
- Zacatecas 1548 SILVER
- Approximate frontier 1540
- Mexico
- to Acapulco
- Havana
- miles 0 — 500
- km 0 — 800

The great conquests: South America

The Incas of Peru

This wooden Inca drinking cup was probably made soon after the Spaniards came to Peru, and is 8¾ in (22 cm) high. The back, shown here, is painted with Inca soldiers brandishing slings and standards. The front is carved in the form of a jaguar's head.

Again, the story of this conquest cannot be told here properly, and we shall have to be content to pick out one or two of the most important features. The hero – or you may think him the villain – of this story was not like Cortes, who was an educated man. Francisco Pizarro was a hard-bitten soldier of fortune who had had to fend for himself as long as he could remember. For many years he had sought his fortune among the islands and in the settlements of the mainland, and had gained nothing but experience. In Panama he heard Indian tales of a great, rich land far to the south, and he believed. With great difficulty he raised the money for expeditions. Twice he failed to reach his goal, though he got far enough to see evidence that there was a great and civilised empire further on. At last, in 1532, Pizarro landed on the coast of Peru, with a tiny army.

The emperor of Peru, Atahualpa, was well informed. As Pizarro marched inland, Atahualpa sent a messenger inviting the Spaniards to visit him. The Spanish force consisted of 62 cavalry and 106 infantry, of whom less than twenty had cross-bows and only three hand-guns. Their road led into the mountains, the towering Andes, along dizzy precipices, over swaying bridges, past stone forts which could have stopped an army ten times the size of Pizarro's. Roads, bridges, forts were well maintained. The empire of Peru was efficient and strong.

The Inca Empire of Peru was probably the most completely organised state that has ever existed.

At the top was the Inca himself, all-powerful, a descendant of the Sun-god.

Next came the chief nobles, all members of the sacred Inca family; these nobles had the most important jobs in the state, and often had to govern different parts of the Inca Empire.

The lesser nobles were the chiefs of tribes that had been conquered by the Incas, and had accepted Inca rule. Like the higher nobles, they were given a thorough training and testing before being allowed to exercise power.

The ordinary people were villagers, working on the land. A man lived and died in his own village, and did not go far from it unless ordered to do so by the government. He had no freedom. He did what he was told, when he was told, and paid his taxes in whatever crops or goods he produced. (It may remind you of the Roman Empire after Diocletian had 'frozen' it.) But the Peruvian peasant, in return, was well looked after. When he got married, the government made sure that he had enough land to support himself and his family. If the crops failed, the government would save him from starvation by opening reserve stores of food which had been prepared against such disasters. A strong army protected him from foreign enemies.

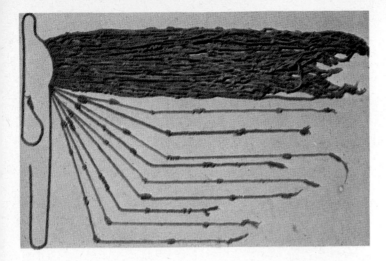

A *quipu*, faded but preserved in the dry atmosphere. It was probably made during the fourteenth or fifteenth century.

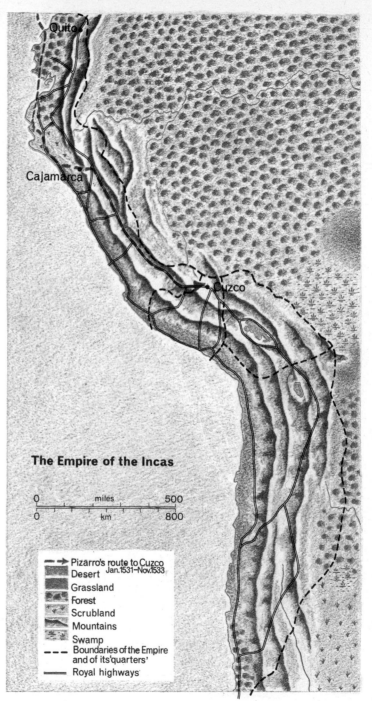

The Empire of the Incas

```
0          miles        500
0          km           800
```

- - - → Pizarro's route to Cuzco
Jan.1531–Nov.1533
Desert
Grassland
Forest
Scrubland
Mountains
Swamp
- - - Boundaries of the Empire and of its 'quarters'
——— Royal highways

Villagers would often have to serve for a time in the army, and then they might be sent to any part of the empire. Sometimes men were needed to help in the building of roads, bridges, temples or forts. Everywhere messengers were needed, and carriers. Like the Aztecs, the Incas had no wheeled vehicles – not that they would have been very useful in the mountains – and the llamas could carry only small loads, slowly. Therefore men had to be ready to carry goods or messages to the next village.

Everything was so tightly controlled that you would expect the government to use papers by the thousand: lists, records, forms, accounts, copies of laws and orders. But the Incas had no way of reading and writing. Instead they had an arrangement of strings, of different lengths and colours, with knots tied in various places. A trained official could understand what a *quipu*, as a set of strings was called, meant. This idea was partly a code, partly a much more elaborate version of the idea of tying a knot in your handkerchief to remind you to do something, for the Inca officials had to be able to remember what the knots stood for.

Running an empire without any means of writing is no more remarkable than building like this without either machinery or iron tools. The size and accuracy of their stone-work has rarely been equalled.

right: Road terraced along the mountain-side and paved; north of Cuzco.

below: Doorway into the sacred enclosure at Pisac.

above: Stairs to the 'lost city' of Machu Picchu. Behind the deserted buildings the steep slopes retain Inca agricultural terraces.

above right: The Spanish church of Santo Domingo in Cuzco has often been damaged in earthquakes, but the Inca masonry below has endured. It was part of the Coricancha (House of Gold), the Temple of the Sun.

right: The fortress of Sacsahuaman (Hawk's Eyrie), overlooking Cuzco, consists of three massive tiers of zig-zag terracing. This is an entrance stair to the first terrace. The upright projecting corner stones are each as tall as a man.

The Mochica irrigated the parched coast of northern Peru, and their civilisation lasted from about A D 400 to 1000. Among the great quantities of excellent pottery which have survived in their graves are many portrait jugs like this.

The capture of Peru

The Inca Empire was not conquered; it was captured. The way in which all power was centred on the Inca meant that to hold the empire it was only necessary to hold the Inca, and this is just what Pizarro did. Atahualpa was so sure of his overwhelming power that Pizarro was able to seize him in a treacherous surprise attack. Then Pizarro could give orders to the whole empire. The only other possible leader of the Peruvians was the imprisoned half-brother Huascar, and Atahualpa himself sent secret orders to have him killed.

Atahualpa tried to bribe his way to freedom. He had noticed the Spanish greed for gold, and thought that it was possible that Pizarro would be so greedy that he would make the mistake of accepting a ransom. Standing in a room which measured seventeen feet by twenty-two – another good authority says thirty-five – he raised his arm as high as he could up the wall. At that height, nine feet, a line was drawn round the room. He promised to fill the room with gold up to that height, and to fill two small rooms with silver, as the price of his liberty.

The treasure arrived, but instead of releasing Atahualpa, Pizarro had him tried and executed on trumped-up charges. It was a disgusting crime, of course, but could Atahualpa ever have seriously thought that Pizarro would dare to let him go? Pizarro set up a brother of Huascar as the new Inca, and was able to go on giving his orders through him. There was no serious attempt to rise against the Spaniards until three years later, and by that time it was too late.

Most of the fighting which took place in Peru was between the Spaniards themselves, who quarrelled about the sharing out of the land. Pizarro defeated and executed his old friend Almagro in 1538, and was himself murdered by supporters of Almagro's son in 1541. When a viceroy was sent by the king of Spain, there was a revolt led by Pizarro's brother, and the viceroy was defeated and killed in 1546. It was not until 1548 that a new viceroy was able to crush the rebels, and at last bring some law and order back to Peru.

Though the people who lived in that part of South America had reached a good level of civilization hundreds of years earlier – this pot, for example, was made in Peru at about the time Charles the Great was trying to rebuild the Roman Empire in Europe – the Inca Empire was only about a hundred years old when the Spaniards came. It had been growing during that hundred years until it had reached the size you saw on the map on page 61, and the whole of this vast territory and its elaborate, tight system of government, depended on one man, the Inca himself. All went well as long as there was nothing wrong with the Inca.

Unfortunately, shortly before the arrival of Pizarro, the system had cracked. There had been a civil war between two half-brothers, Huascar and Atahualpa, for the throne. Atahualpa had won, slaughtered his opponents and imprisoned Huascar. This was the man who, with a large army, awaited the arrival of the Spaniards at a place called Cajamarca.

More conquistadors

Meanwhile, other adventurers were spreading over South America. They endured great hardships, plunging from the heights of the Andes to the jungles of the Amazon and the Atacama desert, always looking for riches and for lands. The map shows the names of the most famous, and where they went.

Within a century of Columbus' first landing, the flag of Spain flew over almost the whole of South America. The men who carried it there are rightly known simply by the Spanish word for conquerors – the conquistadors.

The task of governing

The Portuguese had been the first European nation to make – or take – an overseas empire, but it was mainly a trading empire. Spain was the first country in Europe to get an empire which covered thousands of square miles of land and included millions of coloured people, many of them uncivilised and most with ideas quite different from those of their new rulers.

During the next four centuries, other European countries were to collect overseas possessions, so that the word 'colonies' came to mean something quite different from its meanings in Greek or Roman history. For good or ill, the whole world was to be shaped by this expansion of Europe; many of the most important questions facing the peoples of the world today have been caused by it. Since the Spaniards were the first of the modern colonial powers, they had to try to find out for themselves how to run an empire; they had nobody to copy. Therefore we can learn a great deal, which may help to explain some of our present-day problems, by studying what happened to Spain and the peoples of her empire.

Problems of power

At first the king of Spain and his advisers did not realise what they had let themselves in for. The conquistadors pushed ahead without giving much thought to anything beyond the gamble in which they were staking their lives against the chances of winning fame and riches. As you probably noticed when reading of the conquest of the New World, this was very different from the well-planned building of the Portuguese Empire. The first job of the Spanish government was to catch

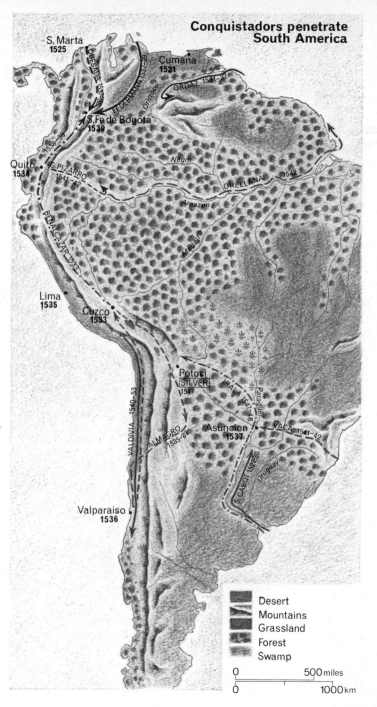

Conquistadors penetrate South America

Desert
Mountains
Grassland
Forest
Swamp

0   500 miles
0   1000 km

up with the conquistadors, and work out a system of governing those vast and distant domains.

The practical problem of taking and keeping a firm grip on conquistadors and Indians alike became more urgent as treasure mines were discovered, the fabulous mines of Potosi and Zacatecas. The king of Spain desperately needed his share of this silver to win the wars in which he was constantly being involved in Europe. Because of these wars, too, he did not have men and money to spare for the New World, to enforce his commands there. He had to rely on the loyalty of the conquistadors.

As it happened, the conquistadors were loyal. In Spain there was a strong feeling that a gentleman, an *hidalgo*, must always serve God and the king; and every conquistador considered himself to be an hidalgo. Besides, only the king could give titles – Cortes became a marquis, Pizarro too – and appoint men to important posts like governorships. Only the king had the power to bestow lands legally, and if a conquistador had brains enough to succeed in fighting he usually had brains enough to see that the only way of being sure of keeping what he had won was to have the right legal documents. Another thing that helped to keep the men in the New World loyal, especially in the early years, was the knowledge that they needed food and wine, clothes and weapons, and reinforcements from Spain. So the king of Spain, even if he was in no position to send soldiers to back up his orders in America, had some hold over the conquistadors.

A department of the Spanish government was set up to deal with America. It was called the Council of the Indies, because the old name given by Columbus lingered long after people knew the truth about the New World. The Council ordered that all ships sailing to 'the Indies' had to use Seville, and no other port. This made it easier to control the trade and to collect the king's dues, such as the royal fifth of all precious metals found in his American lands. In Seville pilots were trained for Atlantic voyages and maps were prepared. Later in the sixteenth century, as the dangers from pirates and

Though drawn in England in the eighteenth century, this diagram of a mine at Potosi gives a fair idea of the methods employed. Many of the miners were Indians conscripted by the government, and a high proportion of these died.

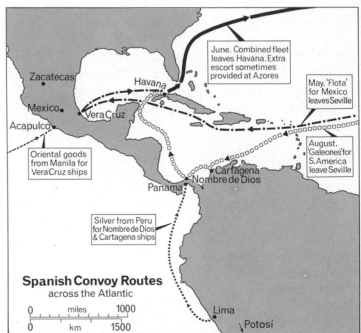

June. Combined fleet leaves Havana. Extra escort sometimes provided at Azores

May. 'Flota' for Mexico leaves Seville

August. 'Galeones' for S. America leave Seville

Oriental goods from Manila for Vera Cruz ships

Silver from Peru for Nombre de Dios & Cartagena ships

Zacatecas

Mexico

Acapulco

Havana

Vera Cruz

Cartagena

Nombre de Dios

Panama

Lima

Potosí

Spanish Convoy Routes
across the Atlantic

0 miles 1000
0 km 1500

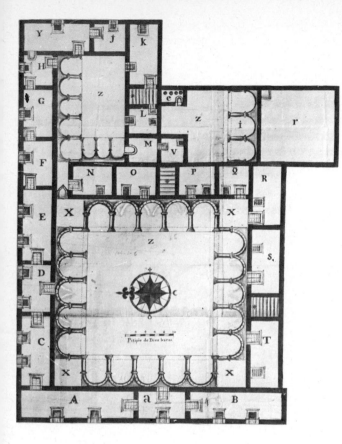

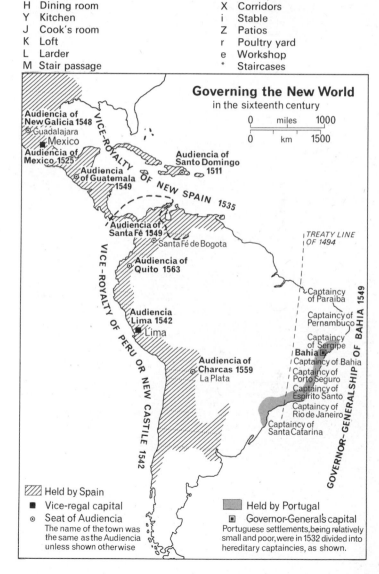

Plan made in 1756 for the palace at Guadalajara, Mexico, where the Audiencia of New Galicia resided.

A Chapel
a Anteroom of the Audiencia
B Courtroom of the Audiencia
C Office of the President
D Anteroom of the President
E Main room
F Bedroom
G Wardrobe
H Dining room
Y Kitchen
J Cook's room
K Loft
L Larder
M Stair passage
N Secretary's room
O Assessor's room
P President's Chaplain's room
Q Audiencia Chaplain's room
R Chancery
S Secretary's office
T Board room
V Fuel store
X Corridors
i Stable
Z Patios
r Poultry yard
e Workshop
* Staircases

Governing the New World
in the sixteenth century

enemies became worse, a convoy system was set up which proved remarkably successful in protecting the valuable cargoes. Of course, other nations were not allowed to trade with South America, and as time went on it became harder to enforce this, and more money had to be spent on defence.

In America itself the Council of the Indies had to entrust its powers to viceroys, who, as you can see from the map, were given wide territories to govern. They had to be given considerable powers if they were to be able to do their difficult job at all, and they had to be chosen very carefully. In fact, some of these viceroys were very wise and strong men. But viceroys and governors were not trusted completely. The map also shows how the empire was covered by *audiencias*. An audiencia was a powerful law court. Its judges had to see that the laws were properly respected by everybody, and they could hear appeals against governors or even viceroys. Appeals could

The front of this house in Potosi displays the wealth and ostentation of its creole builders.

finally be taken beyond both the audiencia judges and the viceroys to the Council of the Indies, in Spain. Thus the Council tried to see that none of the officials in the empire became powerful enough to risk being disobedient.

All important officials were usually Spaniards from Spain. The colonial Spaniards, the descendants of the conquistadors, or *creoles* as they came to be called, wanted everything to be run for their own benefit. It was obvious that these creoles would not often be fair to the Indians, and only complete outsiders could be trusted to put justice first. Audiencia judges, so as to be kept free from being influenced or bribed by the colonial Spaniards, were ordered to mix as little as possible with the creoles, and never to intermarry with them; to make this easier, the judges should live together in a house of their own. On the other hand, in case the officials used their powers badly, each one, after his term of office was over had to remain for some weeks in the place where he had worked. This was to give a chance to anyone who had a complaint against him, but who had been afraid to accuse him while he was in power.

From all this you see how the Spanish government tried to balance everything, so that nobody became too powerful. There were very serious drawbacks. Part of the trouble was that there was not enough money to pay all the officials properly; some became corrupt. There were too many jobs, often badly paid, for the government to be able to find good men to do them; so colonial Spaniards, creoles, often had to be employed in the less important tasks, where they were sometimes discontented and oppressive to the Indians. The biggest weakness, though, was that this care, balancing, making sure that everybody could appeal against everybody else, could lead to tremendous delays. It was much easier to stop than to get anything done. There were so many appeals to the Council of the Indies, and questions, that often it took years before a matter was decided. In the seventeenth century the Spanish government tied itself up, tighter and tighter, in its own rules and regulations. This was one reason why Spain and Spanish America earned the reputation of being places where nothing ever got done, where everything had to wait until *mañana* – 'tomorrow'.

There was another set of results, though. In many ways the system was a great success. Spain held the great bulk of her empire for 300 years. Farms, plantations and ranches were developed, and many manufactures. Towns soon ceased to be collections of shacks. Churches were built and richly adorned. Universities were founded, books published. In the seventeenth and eighteenth centuries Mexico City and Lima could easily match the capital cities of Europe. Spanish America was created.

Spanish colonial churches also displayed great wealth and were built in ornate baroque style, so as to impress people with the splendour of God. The exterior view is of the Jesuit church in Cuzco. This building was begun in 1571 but rebuilt in 1658. The interior view is of the church of San Pedro, Lima, begun in 1613 and completed 1638.

Questions of right

So far we have been thinking of the problems of governing the New World as if it were simply a matter of practical politics between the Spanish government at home and the Spanish creoles in the colonies. But that is only part of the story. It leaves out religion, and it leaves out the subject peoples, the Indians.

Throughout the sixteenth century the rulers of Spain were very religious. They thought that it was their duty to spread their religion among the heathens, just as they thought that they must fight for it against the Muslims in the Mediterranean and, especially in the later part of the century, against the Protestants of Germany, the Netherlands, France and England. They had no doubt that their first duty in America was to convert the Indians to Christianity.

But did this mean that they had the right to use force? There were long arguments.

No responsible man argued that the Indians could be attacked simply because they were heathen, or that they should be forced to become Christians at the point of the sword.

Some said that when the Pope had given his blessing to the division of the world between Portugal and Spain, this meant that those two countries were entitled to conquer the lands of heathens. Most people, however, doubted the Pope's power to give away kingdoms like this.

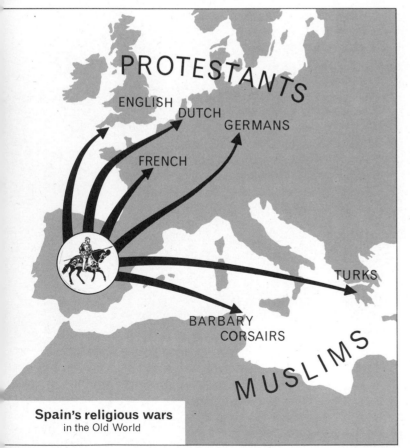

Spain's religious wars
in the Old World

The argument which seemed best to the Spanish government was that force could be used if the Indians refused to allow the missionaries to preach, and particularly if they attacked them. This idea was taken so seriously that conquistadors were ordered not to fight Indians until they had first read out to them an appeal for peace, explaining that the Spaniards wished only to preach to them for their own good. This document was actually read sometimes, but we have no record that it ever prevented the two sides from joining battle – especially as the man reading it had to stand out of range of Indian missiles!

Another strong argument was that the Spaniards could fight to protect their Indian friends, or could intervene to stop the sacrifice of innocent Indians. Some argued that merchants were also entitled to protection from Indians who did not wish to trade with them.

So it was possible to justify many of the conquests, though it is not very likely that most of the conquistadors themselves bothered about the arguments. To them, it was enough to be able to believe – as most of them genuinely did – that they were fighting God's battles against people who were in the throes of devil-worship. Anyway, most of the conquering had already been done before the arguments had been fully considered. A much more important question now was: *What rights had the Indians, once they had been conquered?*

You saw on page 48 how some of the conquistadors acted as if the Indians had no rights at all. Even those who had no share in the cruelties seem to have believed that it was only right and proper for the Indians to work for them. They wished to become lords in the New World, to receive *encomiendas*. An encomienda was rather like a knight's or lord's fief during the Middle Ages, for the man who held it was in charge of Indian towns or villages. The Indians in these towns and villages would support the Spaniard, in return for his protection and his ensuring that they were taught Christianity. This system had its merits. At least it made sure that a good watch was kept on the conquered people, and it rewarded the conquerors. It is difficult to think of anything else which would have worked in the circumstances.

Some of the conquistadors, and their descendants the creoles, would have said that the Indians were naturally inferior to the Spaniards, and that they would always need to be looked after like this. There were even missionaries who wondered if the Indians were fully human, because they found it so hard to talk to them and understand their ways of thinking. One friar went so far as to declare that Indians had no souls, like animals. But his views were condemned by the Church, and he had to withdraw. Most missionaries worked hard to help the Indians.

The Spanish government did not like encomiendas. For one thing, encomienda-holders might become too powerful, standing between the king and the Indians. The government believed that the Indians were the subjects of the king, exactly

as the Spaniards were; they were not the subjects of the colonial Spaniards. They should go on living according to their own customs, provided that these did not seem bad to the king of Spain. They should keep their own chiefs, and of course they must not be robbed, ill-treated or enslaved. That was what the Council of the Indies said, and that was what it meant. It said so most definitely in the famous 'New Laws of the Indies' of 1542, which laid down that all encomiendas must be abolished.

To carry out its orders the government chose many hard-working and courageous officials, and these were generally backed by the power of the Church, too, for the king of Spain had the privilege given him by the Pope of choosing the bishops in his empire. The Spanish government intended to treat the Indians well, and, on the whole, it seemed to have enough power to be able to do so. Now we must see where those good intentions led.

The Indians in New Spain

It is best to look at what happened to the Indians of Mexico, or New Spain as it had been renamed, because most is known about them. It would be wrong to suppose that exactly the same things happened to all the Indians of the New World, because conditions were so different in different parts, but this example shows how easily things could go wrong.

Just after the conquest there was a great deal of confusion. Some conquistadors robbed Indians and worked them to death. After a few years there was better control by the government, and Indians who were badly used could appeal to the judges of the audiencia. Unfortunately, this was not as simple as it sounded. The Indian had to go to the judge, and keep himself alive while he did so; often he could not afford the time, and he did not have the spare food. Sometimes judge and Indian could not properly understand each other. Even if an Indian won his case against a creole, the Spaniard might easily be able to afford the cost of an appeal, and the case could go dragging on. The audiencia courts did the Indians some good – we can be sure of that because of the way some judges were hated by the creoles – but not as much as they were intended to.

When the New Laws of 1542 were announced, there was such an outburst of anger among the men who held encomiendas that the viceroy did not dare to enforce the laws fully, and many years passed before it could be done. (The viceroy was wise: the revolt in Peru which you read about on page 64 was caused by anger against those same laws, and it had led to the death of the viceroy there.) Meanwhile, Spaniards went on obtaining land from the Indians. Sometimes they bought it fairly, sometimes they used threats or bribes because the land did not belong to any one Indian but was the common land of a whole town or village. This could mean that an Indian community would be left without enough land for the people

Portrait of a dedicated official
Luis de Velasco, Marquis of Salinas (1539–1616)
    Viceroy of Mexico 1590–5
    Viceroy of Peru 1596–1604
    Viceroy of Mexico 1607–11
    President of Council of the Indies 1611–16
His father was Viceroy of Mexico 1550–64

to grow their crops. The Indian chiefs were supposed to prevent this sort of thing, but sometimes instead they helped Spaniards to get Indians to labour for them on their farms or in big workshops, where the conditions were not much better than slavery.

As you read on page 71, the Indians were supposed to keep their own laws and customs as much as possible, but even this did not do them much good. Under the Aztecs, as you saw on page 56, they had to pay tribute; they also had to send men to do forced labour on such things as public buildings. This went on in the same way when the Spaniards took over. Often the forced labour was very long and heavy, such as rebuilding Mexico City, draining the lake which had surrounded it, or working in the silver mines; many of the workers died. Taxes, also, became too heavy. The Spanish government had ordered that the Indians should pay less than they had paid under the Aztecs, but Spain needed the money badly and the Indian population was becoming smaller, as so many of them died. Thus, in fact, each Indian had to pay more and more.

This graph shows how the population fell, as far as historians have been able to work it out from the figures which are still available. Why did this happen? There may have been many causes, but the main one was a series of terrible small-pox epidemics, which killed millions of people, as the Black Death had done at times in Europe. Small-pox was a disease which had been unknown before the arrival of the Spaniards, so the Indians were particularly defenceless against it.

Cortes is seated under an awning, with his soldiers behind him. At his side is Marina, the Aztec lady who became his interpreter and adviser. Indian nobles greet him and offer food. This is the sort of treatment to which Spaniards often thought they had a right. The picture is a nineteenth-century copy from a sixteenth-century book made in Tlaxcala, a city famous for its loyalty to the Spaniards.

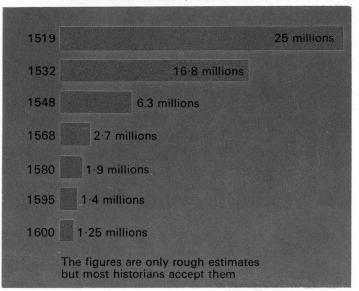

How the Indians of New Spain died after the Conquest

Year	Population
1519	25 millions
1532	16·8 millions
1548	6.3 millions
1568	2·7 millions
1580	1·9 millions
1595	1·4 millions
1600	1·25 millions

The figures are only rough estimates but most historians accept them

In some places the land itself suffered, as a result of the better tools of the Spaniards. They cut down forests with their steel axes, and ploughed the soil much more thoroughly than the Indians could manage with their digging sticks. This sometimes meant that the soil became dusty, and was carried away by winds and streams, particularly when there were no trees to act as shelter. The Spaniards also brought cattle, and these multiplied. Eventually the great herds lived on the ranches of the plains to the north of Mexico, where the land had not been cultivated, but in the early years they did harm to the Indians' crops.

As a consequence of all these things, the Indians of Mexico lost heart; they felt lost and hopeless. Their old civilisation had been swept aside, their old ideas about the gods destroyed. They did not understand their new masters. Disease was striking them down. Their new religion, Christianity, might have given them new hope, but the eagerness of the missionaries probably prevented this from happening as much as it should have done; they baptised Indians in such enormous numbers that most of these new Christians cannot have been properly taught what Christianity really meant.

After about 1600 the Indian population of Mexico stopped shrinking, and gradually began to increase. The worst was over, the first shock had spent itself.

Except that they wiped out the evil religion of the Aztecs, the Spaniards, whatever they had intended, seem to have brought only distress to the Indians of Mexico. The Mexicans today, though their language, religion and most of their civilisation comes from Spain, have not forgotten the long years when the creoles had all the wealth and the Indians suffered. The last Aztec ruler is honoured as a hero, and his statue stands in a prominent place in Mexico City. There is no such statue of Cortes.

Indians, now in European costume, cultivate various plants in a walled garden. A Spaniard, wearing a sword like a gentleman, gives instructions. The picture is by an Indian artist of the 1560s.

A silver 'piece of eight' of 1591. The original is $1\frac{5}{8}$ in (4 cm) in diameter. It was minted at Segovia, indicated by the Roman aqueduct, and its value of eight reales is seen in the VIII. The shield shows what these kings inherited from their Spanish and Burgundian-German ancestors, though not their various possessions in Italy and across the oceans. The inscription reveals that even Spain was not one united kingdom; Philip II was ruler *Hispaniarum* (of the Spains).

The 'Golden Century' of Spain

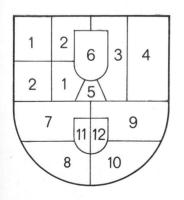

Key:
1 Castile
2 Leon
3 Aragon
4 Sicily
5 Granada
6 Portugal
7 Austria (Habsburg)
8 Burgundy (ancient)
9 Burgundy (modern)
10 Brabant
11 Flanders
12 Tyrol

If the Indians lost, who gained?

Obviously, the conquistadors who survived, and the creoles who inherited their wealth. But these were only a few people.

Did Spain itself gain?

American silver came flowing into the king's treasury. In war after war his armies and fleets were victorious. He humbled France, won and held most of Italy, defended the Catholic Church against the Protestants and the whole of Europe against the Turks. When, in 1580, King Philip II inherited Portugal and the Portuguese Empire, his dominions stretched all round the world. It was a century of glory, and Spaniards have called it the 'Golden Century'.

It is a mistake, though, to confuse size with strength. The Spanish Empire seemed so rich and was so big that others, from pirates to kings, attacked it because they were greedy or because they were afraid that it would grow too strong for anybody else to feel safe. Spain was not a rich country itself, and had not a very large population. The effort to win all those victories was enormous. Philip II went bankrupt three times.

You can see from this that the wealth from America was nothing like enough to pay the bills. It may even have made Spain poorer, because too many people in Spain thought too much of this sort of wealth, and too little of earning wealth by farming, manufacture and trade. Some historians think that the silver from the New World made prices rise so high in Spain that Spanish merchants found it hard to sell their goods, and even in Spain itself people bought goods made in other countries. So Spanish trades and industries began to fail.

The great crash came in the middle of the seventeenth century. Exhausted and defeated at last by her enemies, Spain became a land famous for two things – pride and poverty.

75

In 1570 Abraham Ortelius of Antwerp published what has been called 'the first modern atlas'. His world map shows a great southern land 'not yet known', and sea passages north of both Asia and America. The Atlantic is shown as the central sea, between Old World and New. At this time, of all the nations in the world, only Portugal and Spain held empires across the oceans.

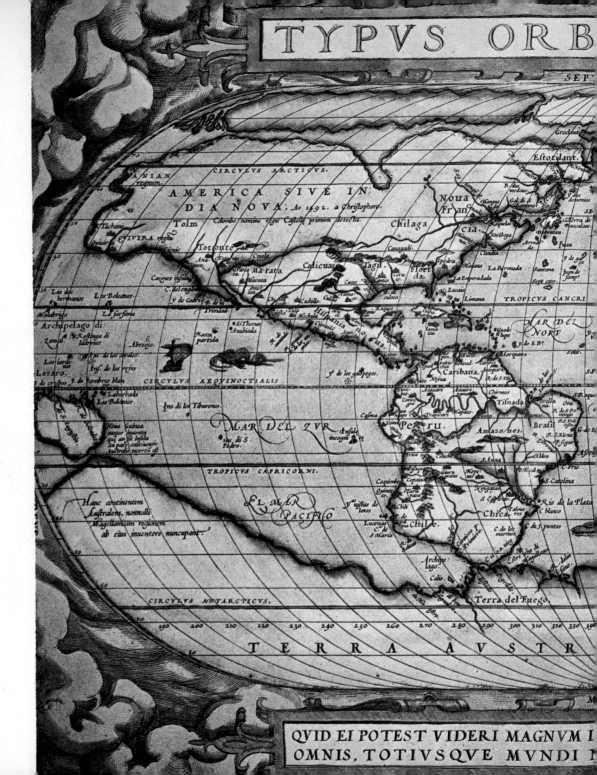

4. COMPETITION FOR COLONIES

New ways to the East

When Portugal and Spain had been dividing up the world, as you read on page 31, the rulers of other European countries had not seemed to care. Venice became alarmed when the Portuguese reached the Indian Ocean, realising that this was a threat to the old trade routes which had brought so much wealth to the Italian cities. The Venetians sent help to the Arabs who tried to defeat the Portuguese but, as you know, the Portuguese won. In the other countries of Europe, though the kings were slow to take an interest, merchants and sailors began to want a share in the wealth from over the oceans.

Trade with the Far East was easily the best way of gaining riches. The problem was how to get there. With the Portuguese

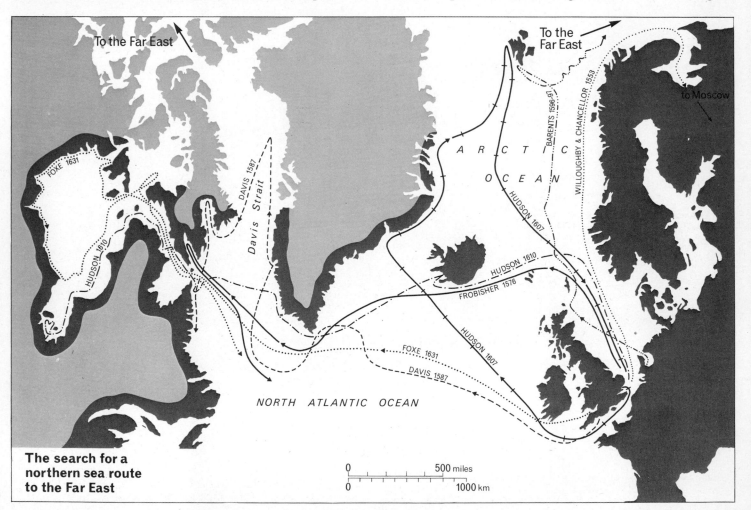

The search for a northern sea route to the Far East

jealously guarding the south-east route, and with the south-west route of Magellan so difficult that the Spaniards themselves did not use it (and they would have blocked it to anybody else, anyway), there remained two more possible routes to be tried: the north-east and the north-west passages.

The map shows what happened. Look at the dates, and you will see that the north-west search, which the Cabots had begun, went on longer than the other. There was so much unknown about North America that it took a long time for hope to fade away. The north-east passage soon seemed hopeless. On both, the explorers at last had to give in to the ice. Some did not give in soon enough. Sir Hugh Willoughby and all his crew died in the ice in 1554, and in 1611 Henry Hudson pushed his men too far, so that they turned him adrift in an open boat.

Both passages did exist. In 1879 the Swedish explorer Nordenskjöld found his way through the ice of the north-east passage, and in 1903 the Norwegian Amundsen did the same in the north-west. Neither passage could be used for trade. It is true that the sixteenth and seventeenth-century sailors who searched for them learned much about the geography of the world, and it was partly because of their work that European colonies were started in North America. But that was not going to make anybody rich.

Pirates, privateers, smugglers and slavers

Long before it became clear that there was no new passage to be found, some sailors had decided that it was quicker and easier to help themselves to a share of what the Spaniards and Portuguese had seized.

The most direct way of doing this was robbery at sea, with or without murder; in other words, piracy. The first cargo of loot which Cortes sent home from Mexico ended its journey in Paris, having been captured by a French ship. But it was not always easy to say whether such captures were plain piracy. If France and Spain, for example, happened to be at war, as they often were, the 'pirate' could claim to be a privateer. This meant that he had permission from his own king to capture enemy ships and sell them. Even in time of peace he might claim that he was only getting his own back for some loss he had suffered previously at the hands of the Spaniards. Excuses like this would not be likely to save him if the Spaniards caught him, but they might be useful if the king of Spain ever complained about him to the king of France.

Other sailors had another idea. They tried to force their way into the trade which Spain and Portugal were trying to keep for themselves. A famous example of this is the story of the Englishman, John Hawkins. His plan was to buy slaves on the west coast of Africa, where the Portuguese authorities would try to stop him, and sell them to the settlers in South America, where the Spanish authorities would try to stop him. Hawkins knew that the settlers would be glad to buy his Negroes if only he could provide them with a good excuse, so that they would not be punished by their own government. Therefore, when he came to a Spanish settlement, he would pretend that he had been driven off his course by bad weather, that he had run short of food and water, and that he had no choice but to sell his slaves. If this story was not enough, he would say that his need was so great that he would be obliged to use force if the settlers refused to trade, and would fire a few shots. Then everybody could carry on trading. He always claimed that he was a friend of the king of Spain, and managed to avoid any real fighting. He may even have thought that eventually he would get permission to trade legally, in return for helping the Spanish government against pirates. Hawkins did very well out of his slave-trading with the Spanish settlers, so well that Queen Elizabeth I invested in his business. But at last, in 1568, he was caught at a disadvantage by a Spanish fleet, and lost most of his ships and men.

One of the results of the defeat of John Hawkins was that English sailors realised that smuggling did not pay, and that they might as well take to open robbery. The best known of these was a young relative of Hawkins, Francis Drake, whose excuse was that he had lost everything in the disaster, and was entitled to compensate himself from the Spaniards.

There is no space here to tell the adventurous life of Francis Drake, and perhaps there is no need. You probably know already the stories of how he raided Spanish America, sailed

The cruelty of the slave trade does not seem to have worried many people in Europe until about 1800, but then there was a movement to put an end to it. This is part of a well-known diagram published then, showing how the slaves were packed for the slow, hot, stinking 'Middle Passage'.

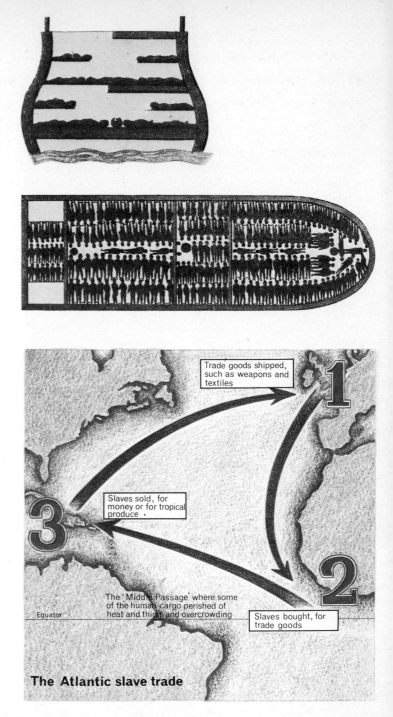

round the world in the *Golden Hind*, and played a big part in defeating the Spanish Armada of 1588. Notice, though, how he began as a small-scale adventurer on his own account and ended commanding the Queen's fleets. He could be described as a pirate or an admiral, or anything in between. He shows us very well how confused and disorderly things were on the oceans in the sixteenth century, and how it is hardly possible to fit such men into neat classes.

From the stories told about the daring exploits of the English 'sea-dogs' of Queen Elizabeth's reign, people often come to think that they all sailed home to Devon, after their raids on King Philip's ships and harbours, with the holds of their ships crammed with treasure. The truth is rather different. As you saw on page 66, King Philip's government had a convoy system which worked very well, and Queen Elizabeth's sailors, though they tried hard, never took one of his treasure ships, let alone a treasure fleet.

There was, however, one really spectacular capture by an English squadron when, after a fierce resistance, the huge *Madre de Dios* was taken. There are full accounts of that ship's almost unbelievably rich cargo. But the *Madre de Dios* was not Spanish. She was Portuguese, and she was coming back from the Far East. It was in the East that the great riches lay. Now that there was open war – for, as you know, Portugal was at this time ruled by the king of Spain, and could be attacked by Spain's enemies – there was no longer any reason why the English should not try to break into the eastern trade which, for a hundred years, the Portuguese had kept to themselves.

The English were not the only ones to see this. The Dutch had been at war with King Philip of Spain for some years, and their bold and determined sailors were also preparing to force their way eastwards.

Trade goods shipped, such as weapons and textiles

Slaves sold, for money or for tropical produce

The 'Middle Passage' where some of the human cargo perished of heat and thirst and overcrowding

Slaves bought, for trade goods

Equator

The Atlantic slave trade

Merchant empires in the East

The Dutch in the East Indies

Dutch ships began trading in the East during the 1590s. In 1595 some merchants clubbed together to form a company, and sent out four ships with about 250 men aboard. After more than two years, the expedition returned, three ships and ninety men. The voyage was counted a great success, as the survivors brough home rich cargoes of spices.

Because of the great profits, many Dutch merchants now formed companies and sent ships to load up in the Spice Islands. In 1601 no less than fourteen squadrons sailed east, a total of sixty-five ships. Soon the merchants and captains saw that it would be safer and easier, especially as they had to try to make treaties with the local kings and fight the Portuguese in the East Indies, if they all worked together.

In 1602 the Dutch government set up the Dutch East India Company. It was to have the 'monopoly' of trading in all the seas east of the Cape of Good Hope and west of the Straits of Magellan. This meant that the Dutch government would not allow anyone to trade there who was not a member of the East India Company. The Company was also given the power to make treaties with kings in that part of the world, and to appoint governors of any trading posts and forts, or 'factories' as they were called then. It goes without saying that ships and

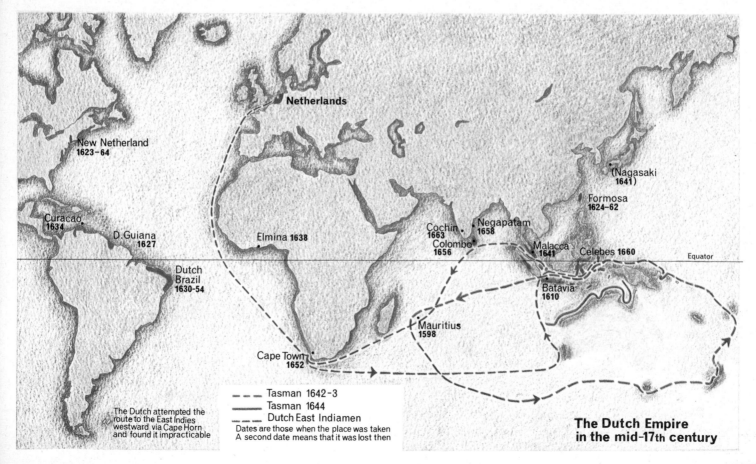

New Netherland
1623–64

Curaçao
1634

D. Guiana
1627

Dutch Brazil
1630–54

Netherlands

Elmina 1638

Cape Town
1652

Mauritius
1598

Cochin
1663
Colombo
1656

Negapatam
1658

Malacca
1641

Batavia
1610

Celebes 1660

Equator

(Nagasaki
1641)

Formosa
1624–62

The Dutch attempted the route to the East Indies westward via Cape Horn and found it impracticable

– – – Tasman 1642–3
——— Tasman 1644
– – – Dutch East Indiamen
Dates are those when the place was taken
A second date means that it was lost then

The Dutch Empire in the mid-17th century

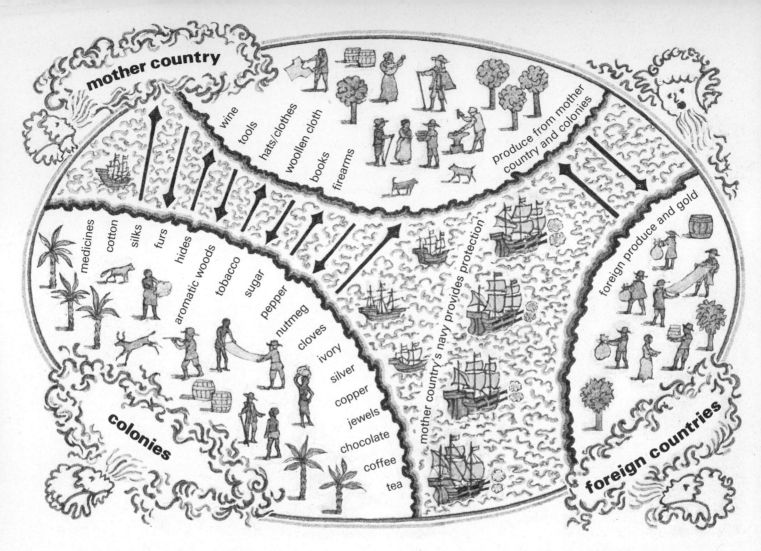

mother country

wine
tools
hats/clothes
woollen cloth
books
firearms

produce from mother country and colonies

medicines
cotton
silks
furs
hides
aromatic woods
tobacco
sugar
pepper
nutmeg
cloves
ivory
silver
copper
jewels
chocolate
coffee
tea

colonies

mother country's navy provides protection

foreign produce and gold

foreign countries

above: The 'Mercantile' Theory. Mother country and colonies supply each other's needs, and with surplus produce the mother country can build up reserves of gold from foreign trade. Gold, it is believed, can always be used to purchase strength and safety.

factories had to be well able to defend themselves, so the Company also appointed admirals and generals.

The Company lost no time in taking all that it could. It made treaties with kings in India, Ceylon and the East Indies. Many of these kings were pleased to see the Dutch attack the Portuguese, who had had everything their own way for so long. Soon it was the Dutch East India Company which was the strongest power in the Spice Islands, and the Dutch had no intention of sharing with anybody else what they had taken from the Portuguese. The English tried to share the trade, but after the so-called 'massacre' at Amboyna in 1623, when

the English merchants were tortured and executed by the Dutch, the English withdrew to India.

By the middle of the seventeenth century the Dutch held a very wide empire. As the map on page 81 shows, it included places in all sorts of climates, with all sorts of pro-

Dutch battleships on a calm day. Notice the inshore fisherman, and the yacht — a new type of fast vessel used for scouting and carrying despatches. The picture was painted by Cornelis van Mooy in 1666.

Two of the hardworking smaller craft on which Dutch prosperity and power really depended. A herring buss (*right*) and a merchant ship (*below right*), both drawn in 1665 by Van de Velde the elder.

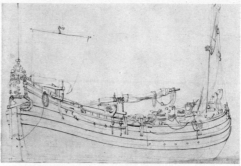

ducts, so that the Dutch would not have to depend on anyone else for goods which could not be grown at home. That was the purpose of colonies in those days — to supply the mother country with whatever she could not produce for herself, and in return to take what she manufactured. The idea, which was part of what has been termed the 'mercantile system' of economics is illustrated opposite. In this way an empire could be self-sufficient. The Dutch succeeded in doing more than this. For many years they controlled the greater part of the sea-borne trade of Europe. Their ships and sailors were so good that most of the trade between the different countries of Europe was carried in Dutch vessels, and much of the coasting trade between different ports in the same country, too. And their fishing fleets were so important that it used to be said that Amsterdam was built on herrings.

The small republic at the heart of this wide commercial empire was wealthy and powerful, far more than its size might suggest. As we saw in the case of Spain, size and strength are not the same. We may be reminded of the wealth and power of Carthage and Venice, both of them republics ruled by merchants, in previous centuries. The seventeenth century was the great century of the Dutch, and, since it was the great age of Dutch artists as well as of merchants and admirals, the people and places have been preserved for us in master-pieces of painting. You have probably often seen pictures like these, either reproduced or in art galleries. When you look at them, remember that these clean, quiet, comfortable people were also the resolute seamen and grim fighters who had taken and held an empire over the oceans.

below left: Boy bringing Pomegranates painted about 1660 by Pieter de Hooch (1629– after 1684). From the shaded room we look across the sunlit courtyard, tiled and clean, of a prosperous house to the street beyond. The fruit must have come from a distant land.
below: Constantijn Huygens and his Clerk painted in 1627 by Thomas de Keyser (1596/7–1667). Huygens (1596–1687) was well-born, wealthy, a diplomat and statesman, poet, artist and athlete. His son Christiaan became a famous astronomer and mathematician.

right: The Avenue at Middelharnis painted in 1689 by Meindert Hobbema (1638–1709). A peaceful road in the flat Dutch countryside, and a man walking his dog.

below right: The Harpsichord Lesson painted by Jan Steen (1626–1679). A scene in a comfortably-off Dutch household.

below: Wigstand, made of Delft earthenware about 1680, and decorated with 'Chinese' figures. Both the purpose and the decoration show what was fashionable then.

Details of a cotton bedspread embroidered with silk in chain-stitch. From Cambay, Gujarat, about 1600. The whole spread is 10 ft 9 in × 8 ft 6 in (3·3 × 2·6 m).

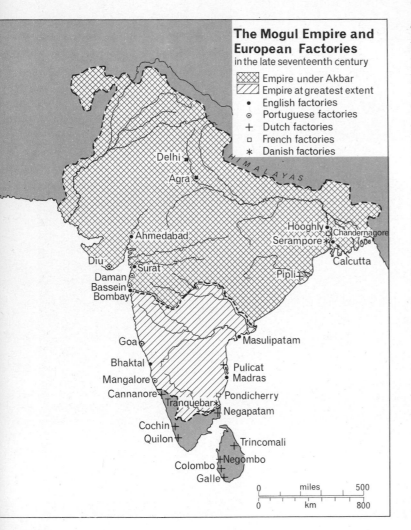

The Mogul Empire and European Factories
in the late seventeenth century

- ⊠ Empire under Akbar
- ⊘ Empire at greatest extent
- • English factories
- ⊙ Portuguese factories
- + Dutch factories
- □ French factories
- ✳ Danish factories

Delhi
Agra
HIMALAYAS
Ahmedabad
Hooghly Chandernagore
Serampore
Calcutta
Diu
Surat Pipli
Daman
Bassein
Bombay
Goa Masulipatam
Bhaktal
Pulicat
Mangalore Madras
Cannanore
Pondicherry
Tranquebar
Negapatam
Cochin
Quilon Trincomali
Negombo
Colombo
Galle

0   miles   500
0   km   800

'Factories' in India

The English East India Company had been founded two years before the Dutch, and English ships had visited the Spice Islands, until they were driven away. Meanwhile, other English ships had been visiting India; here the supply of spices was not so good as in the East Indies islands, but some could be bought, together with such valuable goods as calico and muslin, saltpetre, and indigo and other dyes. India, therefore, even if it had not been their first choice, was an excellent place for establishing trading centres.

As you saw on page 38, the presence of a few European traders on the coast was not particularly important to the great kings who ruled large parts of India. Certainly those powerful monarchs did not think of the merchants as a threat to their own kingdoms, and were often quite willing to allow them to set up trading depots, either in or near Indian ports, and to build defences to protect their goods and themselves. There was nothing very strange in this. You may remember how the Hanseatic merchants during the later Middle Ages had been given similar privileges in different European kingdoms, including England.

The map shows how these 'factories' were placed around the Indian coast during the seventeenth century. Of the four nations who had most of these places, the Portuguese were not as vigorous as they had been, and lost some of their posts to the Dutch or English. The Dutch and English East India Companies were keen traders. The French East India Company was not founded until 1664, and the French merchants did not prove to be nearly as keen as their rivals, so that the French Company had to be encouraged and controlled much more than the Dutch and English Companies by its government at home.

Silver-mounted ivory cabinet, 9½ in (24 cm) high, made in Ceylon about 1700. The carvings of Adam and Eve are copied from a Dutch engraving.

below left: This type of cabinet is Italian, but the inlaid decoration of ivory and bone is Mogul. The cabinet was made soon after 1600, probably in Sind, and measures 26 in (66 cm) across.

below: Portrait of a European painted about 1590 by a Mogul artist.

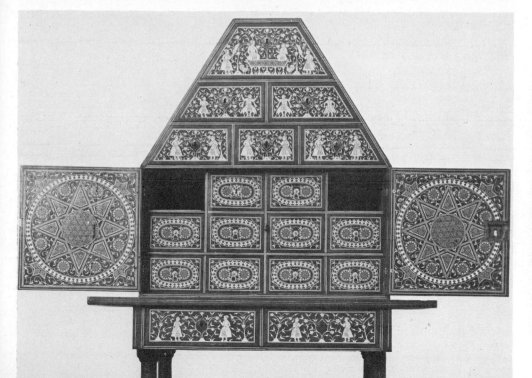

The Mogul Empire

During the years when the Companies were establishing their 'factories', a large part of India was ruled by a dynasty of Muslim emperors. They were known as the Moguls because they originally came from central Asia, the land of the Mongols; in fact, they were descendants of Tamerlane. Like all the invaders of India, the first of the Moguls, Babar, had entered India from the north-west. He died in 1530, after founding an empire in northern India. This empire grew. The greatest of the Mogul emperors was Barbar's grandson, Akbar, who ruled from 1562 to 1605, but the empire became larger still after his death, and was at its largest under Aurangzeb who ruled from 1658 to 1707.

As you may see from these pictures, this was a time of luxury and elegance, at least for the rulers of the empire. Architects and painters created works of charm and delicacy, the most famous of all being the Taj Mahal.

Some historians have thought that, besides the military strength and the artistic splendour, the Mogul Empire should be remembered for having tried to bring unity to India. Akbar saw no reason why the different religions should not live in peace, not only Hindus and Muslims, but Christians also. Later emperors did not have his wide vision, and tried to unite India by the sword alone. They did not succeed. After the death of Aurangzeb the power of the Moguls crumbled, and in the confusion which followed there were new dangers and new opportunities for the European merchants in their factories.

above: 'A dream in marble'. The Taj Mahal was built at Agra in 1632 by Akbar's grandson, Shah Jehan, as a mausoleum for his favourite wife, Mumtaz Mahal.
left: In 1569 Akbar founded the city of Fatehpur Sikri as a thank-offering for the birth of his son. This picture shows him inspecting its building. It comes from a manuscript 'Life of Akbar' of about 1590.

One of Aurangzeb's generals. Aurangzeb, who deposed his father Shah Jehan in 1658 was the last really powerful Mogul emperor.

far right: A feast at court from a Mogul painting made about 1620.

right: Washing clothes and drawing water, from a manuscript of about 1680.
far right: Weaving, from a manuscript of about 1680.

left: The mausoleum of Prince Itimad-ud-Daula at Agra. Completed in 1628, it is of white marble covered with mosaic.

The furthest East

It may have occurred to you that, after there had been so much European interest in China during the thirteenth century and after Columbus had looked for China and Japan in the West Indies, it is odd that we have heard so little about the most distant East. The reasons for this, though, are not difficult.

First, look at the position through the eyes of the traders from the different European countries. What they mostly wanted was spices, and they could get them without going as far as China – that is, if they were coming from the West. The long voyage across the Pacific from Spanish America was very difficult. The most valued produce of China was silk, and not many ships were needed to carry a large amount of this. Therefore, the Portuguese at Macao and the Spaniards at Manila (from which a large ship sailed each year with an enormously valuable cargo for Mexico and, eventually, Europe) were able to handle all the trade for which there was any great demand.

It is just as important to look at the position as it seemed to the Chinese and Japanese.

You have already seen how the Chinese thought that they had nothing to gain by contact with foreigners (see pages 15 and 17) and probably most of the Europeans who reached China during the sixteenth century made the Chinese authorities even more sure that the foreigners were inferior. The mandarins, trained in the old traditions, did not look upon the pursuit of wealth as a very honourable occupation; and most of the Europeans they met were pursuing wealth very hard indeed, some of them being more pirates than merchants. Therefore Europeans were kept out of China, and only allowed to trade in one or two places. A few Christian missionaries were allowed to live at the Imperial Chinese court, especially Catholic priests of the Society of Jesus. But these men were admitted because of their great learning, and because in many scientific matters, from astronomy to gardening, they showed themselves to be wiser than the learned men of China. Besides, they dressed and spoke like educated Chinese. Even these men, however, were not allowed to go freely about China.

We must remember, too, something that ought to be obvious. Compared to the other matters which the government of China had to deal with, Europe was of very little importance.

The Exclusive Empires

JAPAN

Nagasaki
(Dutch factory 1641, under strict supervision)

N

CHINA

FORMOSA
(Dutch 1624, driven out 1662)

Macao
(Portuguese 1555)

PHILIPPINES (Spanish)

Manila
(1571)

– – – Portuguese and Spanish route to Europe via Acapulco

········· Dutch route to Europe via Malacca

0   500 miles
0   500   1000 km

The Shoguns of Japan

Though the Japanese may have owed much of their civilisation to China in the beginning, they had developed many ideas of their own. There is no need to say much about the look of old Japan. Most of us have often seen pictures of Japanese in their traditional costume, or of Japanese houses or temples. One reason why it is so easy to see photographs of these things is that the Japanese, perhaps more than any other nation in the world, like keeping to their old traditions as much as they can, in the midst of all their modern commerce and industry.

In the times we are thinking about, the Japanese were a particularly warlike nation – or, rather, the most important class of Japan were. These men were called Samurai, and they believed that fighting was the only honourable way of making a living. (You will be able to think of other peoples who, at various times, had similar ideas.) The great nobles of Japan kept Samurai to fight for them, and it is not surprising that there was often lawlessness and civil war in Japan.

The emperor, the Mikado, to use the title by which he is usually known in English, was thought to be descended from the sun. Such a belief, as you have seen, gave the Inca great power over the Peruvians, but it did not work like that in Japan. Instead, the emperor was often treated as being outside the rough-and-tumble of practical life, and great nobles ruled the country for him. For centuries the most powerful man in Japan was the officer known as the 'Shogun', who was a kind of permanent president ruling on behalf of the emperor. After many years of civil wars, in 1600 the Tokugawa family managed to make themselves Shoguns. They were determined to hold on to power (in fact they did, until 1868) and not to allow anything to disturb Japan.

Thus the Japanese government was suspicious of foreigners. Would they cause trouble? Portuguese and Spanish missionaries were beginning to have a good deal of success in converting Japanese to their religion. Did this mean that there was a plot to take over Japan for the king of Spain? There began a persecution of the Christians, which became worse until Christianity in Japan was wiped out.

Foreign traders were also dangerous, it seemed. They might be playing the same sort of game as the missionaries. Anyway, the merchants of the different European nations were always quarrelling and accusing one another. Thinking like this, the Shogun decided that Japan must be cut off from the outside world, and in the 1630s this is what he did.

All foreigners were expelled. Only the Dutch were allowed to trade, at one small island in Nagasaki Bay, and by the eighteenth century they were allowed to send only two ships per year. These, and a few Chinese merchants in Nagasaki, were the only outsiders who had any contact with Japan. At the same time, Japanese were not allowed to go abroad; any who did go, even if accidentally driven by storms, were not to return. No large ships were to be built. Japan raised the drawbridge, and kept it up for two centuries.

Model of Honda Tadakatsu (1548–1610), a general who helped to establish Ieyasu, first of the Tokugawa shoguns. He wears full samurai equipment which may at first sight seem complicated and clumsy but is in fact very effective. At this period samurai normally fought on foot. The model was made early in the twentieth century for the Japanese Boys' Festival, and stands 22 in (56 cm) high.

New powers in America

The sugar islands

Compared with the wealth from the East, there was not much to be gained from the New World after the Spaniards had taken the most attractive parts. Not much, that is, for merchants. But another idea was beginning to make the governments of various countries in Europe want to establish colonies. This was the idea you met on page 83, that no self-respecting country ought to depend on any other country for anything that was really necessary: food, or minerals, or munitions of war. This, of course, included tropical crops, like spices and now sugar.

Sugar originally grew in the East, but the Spaniards had brought the plant to the Caribbean islands. It was grown on plantations, and it needed a large number of workers. Since the work was not very skilled and was easily supervised, slave labour was cheapest. Since, as you know, the Indians of the islands died out, Negroes were brought from West Africa.

Many of the islands had no Spanish settlers. Others had only a few. Anyway, there were far too many islands in the West Indies for the Spaniards to be able to defend when the other countries of Europe began to want sugar-growing islands for themselves. An example: in 1655 the English admiral Penn tried to take Hispaniola, but was driven away. So he went to Jamaica, where there were only a few Spanish settlers, and was able to capture that island. By the end of the seventeenth century many islands were owned by other European nations, as the map shows.

During the years when these other nations had been breaking into the seas which Spain had tried to keep for herself, there had been a lot of disorder, and the Caribbean had been the home of the notorious 'buccaneers'. At first these men were mostly French, and claimed that they were only peaceful sailors and hunters who had settled in some of the uninhabited islands, had been attacked by the Spaniards, and

were trying to make up for the losses they had suffered. In fact, they behaved as pirates who mainly attacked Spanish ships and towns. These buccaneers were very brave, desperate fighters. They were also hideously cruel. When things became more settled in the West Indies, after the French and English had taken a firm grip on their islands and now wanted peace and order, the buccaneers found that they could no longer count on their help. They were given the choice of retiring or being treated as pirates. The most famous of them, Henry Morgan, saw that times had changed, submitted to King Charles II of England, was knighted in 1675 and became Governor of Jamaica, where it was his duty to put down any buccaneers who still thought that they could live by violence.

The sugar islands prospered. Labour was very cheap. Negro slaves were plentiful, and therefore their owners did not need to treat them very well. They were forced to work hard, and the punishment of those who rebelled against their brutal treatment was ferocious: severe flogging normally, and sometimes being cut to pieces or being hung up alive, to die of hunger, thirst and pain.

The planters who grew rich on this slave labour were able to live like some of the slave-owners in ancient times, in luxury and elegance.

The mainland of North America

North America had fewer attractions than other parts of the New World. True, there was the possibility that gold or silver *might* be found, but the Spanish expeditions had been unsuccessful, and everybody knew it. True, an easy way to the Far East *might* be found, but you saw on page 79 that the search for the north-west passage was not going well. But there were other reasons for founding settlements there. Since the English founded more colonies than the other European nations in North America, we should probably learn most by studying their reasons.

In the time of Queen Elizabeth I, some men had thought that English ships would never be able to attack Spanish America and the treasure fleets successfully until they had a base on that side of the Atlantic. Both the French and the English had tried in vain to found such settlements in the later part of the sixteenth century, and the idea lingered on after

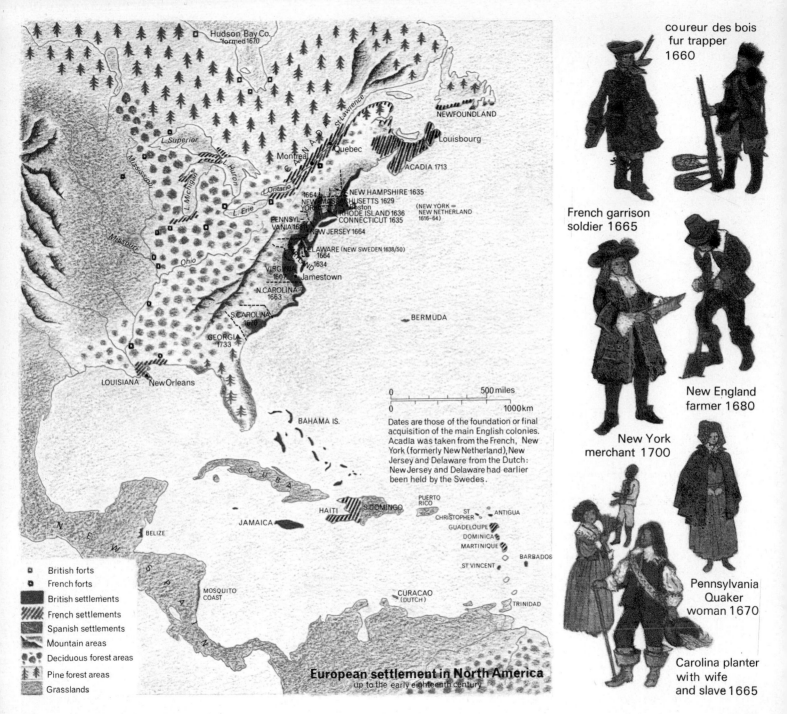

Hudson Bay Co. formed 1670

NEWFOUNDLAND

L. Superior

L. Michigan

L. Huron

L. Ontario

L. Erie

St Lawrence

Montreal   Quebec   Louisbourg

ACADIA 1713

Mississippi

Missouri

Ohio

C A N A D A

1664   NEW HAMPSHIRE 1635
NEW   MASSACHUSETTS 1629
YORK   Boston
        RHODE ISLAND 1636
PENNSYL-   CONNECTICUT 1635
VANIA 1681   NEW JERSEY 1664
            DELAWARE (NEW SWEDEN 1638/50)
            1664
MARYLAND 1634

(NEW YORK = NEW NETHERLAND 1616–64)

VIRGINIA 1607   Jamestown

N. CAROLINA 1663

S. CAROLINA 1670

GEORGIA 1733

LOUISIANA   New Orleans

BERMUDA

BAHAMA IS.

N   E   W

S   P   A   I   N

BELIZE

MOSQUITO COAST

CUBA

JAMAICA   HAITI   S. DOMINGO   PUERTO RICO
                                ST
                                CHRISTOPHER   ANTIGUA
                    GUADELOUPE
                        DOMINICA
                        MARTINIQUE
                                    BARBADOS
                ST VINCENT

CURACAO
(DUTCH)   TRINIDAD

0   500 miles
0   1000 km

Dates are those of the foundation or final
acquisition of the main English colonies.
Acadia was taken from the French, New
York (formerly New Netherland), New
Jersey and Delaware from the Dutch:
New Jersey and Delaware had earlier
been held by the Swedes.

European settlement in North America
up to the early eighteenth century

- □ British forts
- ◊ French forts
- ▓ British settlements
- ▨ French settlements
- ▤ Spanish settlements
- ⛰ Mountain areas
- ❦ Deciduous forest areas
- 🌲 Pine forest areas
- ▦ Grasslands

coureur des bois
fur trapper
1660

French garrison
soldier 1665

New England
farmer 1680

New York
merchant 1700

Pennsylvania
Quaker
woman 1670

Carolina planter
with wife
and slave 1665

93

peace had been signed in 1604 between England and Spain. Naval experts also pointed out that there was a great need for what were called 'naval stores' – timber of certain kinds, hemp, flax, tar. England had to depend on countries around the Baltic Sea for most of her naval stores, and it seemed likely that many of the right types of timber, at least, might be found in North America. Finally there was the problem of over-population. During the Tudor period in England there had been much unemployment; roads and parts of the big towns had been infested with rogues and vagabonds, cheats, robbers and beggars. It seemed that the country simply had more people than it could support. Just as, 2000 years earlier, over-population had caused some of the Greek city-states to send out colonies, some statesmen thought that the best solution was to send people overseas; only, unlike the Greeks, they intended that the colonies should be kept firmly under the control of the mother country.

Companies were formed and were given royal charters to establish and run colonies. The map on page 93 shows where and when the colonies were founded. Some of the colonists had a motive which we have not mentioned yet: they wanted to worship in ways which the English Church would not permit. This is important. Here is a new sort of colonist. These people were not gold-hungry adventurers and they were not missionaries trying to save the souls of the heathen Indians. They were anxious only to be able to live and pray in their own way, without interference.

Whatever their motives, the settlers had to earn their living in this strange land. Naturally, there were farmers and crafts-men and traders in all the colonies. But, because of differences in land and climate, and also differences in the sorts of people who went there, the way of life in the northern and the southern colonies was not the same. In the north, New England as it was called, the people mostly lived in villages and worked on their own small farms. In Virginia and the other southern colonies rich men began plantations, worked by Negro slaves, growing tobacco.

There were two more sets of English people with interests in North America, the fishermen who sailed to the Newfound-land Banks, and the trappers and traders who worked from the isolated posts of the Hudson Bay Company. But these men were not founding settled colonies.

The English were not the only nation to take an interest in

Fort Pentagoet, a French military post on the border of Acadia, as it may have looked about 1670. The bastioned pattern of European fortifications of the time has been adapted to wilderness conditions.

North America. There had been a Swedish settlement on the Delaware, which was taken over by the Dutch, and then their New Amsterdam was taken by the English and renamed New York. After this, the only European country, apart from Spain, which could rival England in North America was France.

The map shows what a different pattern was made by the French colonies. The English had just landed on the coast and moved inland as they needed more farm land. The French sailed up the St Lawrence; here they founded a small colony called Canada, and farmed by the side of the river. Those who penetrated into the heart of the continent, discovered the Great Lakes and made long canoe voyages down the rivers, were not farmers but trappers and traders, men who found it easy to make friends with the Indians. There were never nearly as many French colonists in North America as there were English, yet the French spread over far greater distances. After the colony of Louisiana had been founded, French trading posts and forts stretched along the great waterways from the mouth of the St Lawrence to the mouth of the Mississippi. Sooner or later, if the English colonies went on expanding towards the west, they would meet the French.

Neither the English nor the French had the same difficulty as the Spaniards in deciding how to treat the Indians. Except near Quebec, Montreal and New Orleans, the French did not interfere very much with the Indians; rather, they shared the Indian way of life, hunting and trapping. The English, taking the land to farm for themselves as they needed it, simply drove the Indians out or killed them.

World History begins

Nowadays we live in one small world. Every part of it is always in contact with every other part.

Before the events you have read about in this book the world was not one; it was only a lot of separate parts. Most nations had not even heard of the existence of many of the others. Great civilisations had grown up having little or no contact with other civilisations; some of them were quite unknown to any other civilised people. That is the picture shown on the first map on page 96.

The other map shows how, by the middle of the seventeenth century, the world was being linked together by the ships of a few European nations. They were not yet bringing the other peoples of the world to know one another, but they were bringing them all, gradually, to know Europe. World history was just beginning.

The way in which it was begun exerted a great effect upon the way it went on, and upon the way it still goes on. Some of the nations of Europe had taken the lead. They were to hold on to it, even to increase it until it almost looked as though white men were the masters of the whole world. You have seen in this book how some were only traders, others missionaries; but how some conquered vast lands and millions of people of other races, while in other lands Europeans destroyed the native peoples and settled in their lands. In these ways many of the important states of the present-day world began to take shape.

In Europe itself there were great consequences. You have seen how some countries became rich and energetic, either in commerce or in war, or both. From this time onwards the rise and fall of European countries was often closely tied to their trade or their empires beyond the seas.

Why was it Europe which found the world? Why not China or India, or one of the Muslim countries, or one of the civilisations of America? There are several possible answers, but there is one which stands out so much that you must have thought of it many times in this book. It is this. In many practical things, especially connected with seafaring and warfare, the European nations were stronger than people of other civilisations. At the same time, they desired the goods produced in other parts of the world more than the people of other civilisations desired European goods. At least, this was true at first. Later, there were new manufactures, machines and inventions which changed the picture, and it may well have been trade with the rest of the world which encouraged Europeans to become so inventive. But that is another story.

Perhaps the discovery of these new lands and seas, new peoples, plants and animals had an even more important influence upon Europeans. Did it provide new facts for the scientists, to stir their minds and make them think of new ideas? Did it arouse the imaginations of artists, of poets and writers of all kinds? Did it suggest opportunity, the chance of more freedom, of independence to thousands of ordinary men and women? Some historians believe that the discoveries set all sorts of people's minds working in fresh ways, and led to vital new ideas in literature, in art, in science, in politics – in practically everything. What happens in men's minds, how ideas are born, is something that we cannot measure and explain exactly, though we all know that it is tremendously important. The astronauts may owe more than they will ever realise to Columbus, Magellan and the rest of the great navigators.

As for the lesser effects which the discoveries had on the daily life of people today – anyone who enjoys tea or coffee, sugar or chocolate, potatoes or tobacco, or a turkey at Christmas ought to think kindly of Henry the Navigator and the men of many nations who took the road he had pointed out.

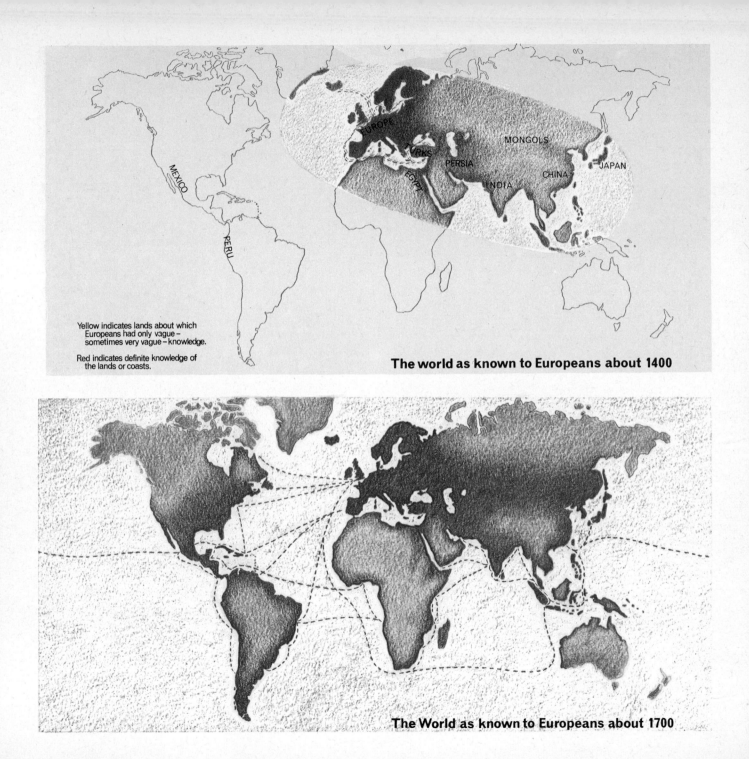

Yellow indicates lands about which
Europeans had only vague –
sometimes very vague – knowledge.

Red indicates definite knowledge of
the lands or coasts.

MEXICO

PERU

EUROPE

TURKS

EGYPT

PERSIA

INDIA

MONGOLS

CHINA

JAPAN

The world as known to Europeans about 1400

The World as known to Europeans about 1700